READING BOILEAU

volume 15

READING BOILEAU

An Integrative Study of the Early *Satires*

Robert T. Corum, Jr.

Purdue University Press
West Lafayette, Indiana

02 01 00 99 98 5 4 3 2 1

∞The paper used in this book meets the minimum requirements of American National Standard for Information Sciences—Permanence of Paper for Printed Library Materials, ANSI Z39.48-1992.

Printed in the United States of America
Design by Anita Noble

Library of Congress Cataloging-in-Publication Data
Corum, Robert T.
Reading Boileau : an integrative study of the early "Satires" / Robert T. Corum, Jr.
p. cm. — (Purdue studies in Romance literatures ; v. 15)
Includes bibliographical references and index.
ISBN 1-55753-110-2 (cloth : alk. paper)
1. Boileau Despréaux, Nicolas, 1636-1711. Satires. I. Title. II. Series.
PQ1721.S32C67 1997
841'.4—dc21 97-16246
CIP

Contents

Introduction

> *Within the closed system of Classical aesthetic-moral values, [satire] allowed the author a certain free play. Through it, he might give vent to his humors and could come closest to self-expression, even though it was self-expression channeled in certain directions and given an accepted form. In this respect the* Satires *of Boileau deserve special attention, for close reading may well give invaluable insight into the mentality of the author and the* métier *of the writer of the time.*
>
> Rémy Saisselin
>
> *The Rules of Reason and the Ruses of the Heart*

The legend of Boileau as the codifier of French classical precepts, although demolished a century ago, has nonetheless encouraged a widespread disdain for his poetic art.[1] By rejecting an aesthetic preoccupation with poems, the theoretician's preoccupation with poetics had made Nicolas Boileau-Despréaux into a venerable national and cultural institution for the advancement of classical doctrine. While the myth provided an uncomplicated unity to the classical movement and a convenient function for its best-known critic, its destruction necessitated a thorough reevaluation of Boileau's real importance in French literary history. Despite an abundant bibliography accumulated over many generations and spanning three centuries of diverse literary standards and principles, relatively few studies of Boileau have focused rigorous critical attention on whole poems in an attempt to uncover and illuminate his art.

In one of the first books assessing the artistic value of Boileau's poetry, Gustave Lanson deplored the fact that the poet of the early *Satires* had been read solely as a moralist and literary theorist.[2] The eminent nineteenth-century scholar quotes isolated verses to bolster his argument that Boileau's chief distinction is his prosodic talent. Lanson's enthusiasm for Boileau's brilliant versification, however, blinds him to the semantic shadings of the satirist's poetic language: "Il choisit ses mots, non comme signes, mais comme sons, et par les rimes, les coupes, les rythmes, il s'efforce de donner au vers une forme sensible capable de susciter une impression déterminée" (50). Lanson also praises Boileau's gifts as a descriptive poet, and points out his precise and evocative observations of the external world. On the minus side, Boileau's lack of decorum and sincerity, and his want of "aucun élément sensible ni moral" (64), exclude him from the ranks of the truly great classical poets. Lanson charges that the *Satires* are without coherence, and hence suggests that ultimately they have limited genuine aesthetic worth:

> En réalité, l'idée générale est peu de chose pour Boileau: l'important pour lui, ce sont les couplets, les images qu'elle relie. Et nulle part, la pièce ne fait tant d'effet que lorsque l'idée générale se laisse oublier à force d'insignifiance et de banalité. Alors chaque morceau nous plaît en soi, détaché de l'ensemble où il n'est logé que par accident et par artifice . . . (66–67)

Many subsequent judgments of Boileau have diverged little from these views: Boileau's poetic gifts lie in his realistic depiction of the concrete and the trivial and in his acrobatic and clever versification. Boileau's defects, however, are serious. He is "incapable de la moindre création" (R. Bray, *Boileau* 163), lacks imagination, and his poems are incoherent, "composed of a series of tableaux of picturesque description" (White 88). These conclusions arise for the most part from the assumption that a valuable poem must express a genuinely felt emotion. In their efforts to emphasize particular passages that appear to illustrate Boileau's descriptive and prosodic virtuosity as well as his perceived insincerity, many commentators have fragmented the texts.[3] Boileau's detractors have also assumed that his poetic language is one-dimensional, practically devoid of figurative undertones. The disregard of poetic wholes and the neglect of linguistic resonances have inevitably led to the charge of incoherence.

Despite the preponderance of impressionistic and nonholistic Boileau criticism, a number of critics have shown a positive bias toward ahistorical, textually centered evaluation. E. B. O. Borgerhoff's indispensable study, *The Freedom of French Classicism,* set the tone by moving away from Boileau's traditional status as a narrowly focused literary critic to insist on his undogmatic doctrine and poetic gifts. Borgerhoff later affirmed in another major contribution that Boileau's poetry presents an exercise in artistic duplicity in which the satiric *je* alternately represents a pseudo-Boileau and Boileau himself.[4] In an analysis of *Satire IX,* Allen G. Wood modified Borgerhoff's "boileau-not-boileau polarity," asserting that two pseudo-Boileaus alternate: the censor and the poetic *persona.*[5] Nathan Edelman further advanced Boileau criticism with his insistence on recurrent, thematically significant, antithetical images of tension/repose, movement/rest, and wakefulness/sleep in Boileau's most famous poem.[6] In another extension of Borgerhoff's work, Jules Brody emphasized that for Boileau poetic creation was primarily a verbal quest. Consequently, the critic must carefully examine his use of language:

> Une lecture de Boileau qui ne reconnaît pas la prééminence du non-discursif et du figuré constituerait une dérogation fondamentale aux exigences de la bonne méthode, qui consiste à essayer d'expliquer les auteurs non à partir d'intentions putatives, mais sur la base de démarches linguistiques effectivement accomplies. ("Boileau et la critique" 241)

Brody's stress on poetic language leads us to rewarding methodological alternatives to the work of earlier critics. One such avenue is suggested by Cleanth Brooks's now classic work, *The Well Wrought Urn.*[7] Brooks's formalist method avoids the analysis of fragments and focuses on whole poems, rigorously examining poetic language to prove that the coherence of many English poems derives from implied metaphors or analogies dispersed through the text. The structural unity of a poem depends upon the blending and harmonizing of apparently disparate, indeed contradictory, connotations and meanings. The language of poetry thus emerges as a "language of paradox" that discloses under meticulous scrutiny a "pattern of resolved stresses." The poetic structure is "a pattern of resolutions and balances and harmonizations, developed through a temporal scheme" (203). For Brooks, the poetic word can be examined only within the context of the total structure and must be seen as polyvalent, containing a cluster of potential meanings that the critic interprets in light of the rest of the poem. The meaning of the poem converges around key words and images whose relationship to the whole is essential. The use of similar critical principles can also demonstrate the coherence of Boileau's poetry.

To illustrate further modern scholarship's evolving position on Boileau, Joseph Pineau's judicious review of past criticism in his recent book grants special credit to American and English commentators, just as Bernard Beugnot and Roger Zuber did some twenty years earlier. These efforts to discover Boileau's aesthetics prompt Pineau to posit a formalist critical model that aims to delve into the "structure fondamentale d'une grande œuvre," within which lies a "nœud bien tressé; le travail du critique est de dénouer la tresse et de montrer comment se forme le nœud" (Pineau 10). In pursuing this crucial objective so often deferred in prior research, the present study proposes close readings of Boileau's first ten published poems, *Satires I–IX* and the *Discours au Roy.*

My assumption is that Boileau is much more than a gifted and acerbic versifier or a strait-laced mouthpiece for classical doctrine. Furthermore, detailed study of individual poems suggests that this youthful *œuvre* can be viewed collectively as a coherent work, just as the poetry books of Boileau's predecessors Horace and Juvenal have been judged as such among Latin scholars.[8]

If we accept the supposition that exacting analysis of whole poems may bring us new insights into a poet's work, a similar holistic approach applied to poetic collections may produce equally valuable results. We should look upon poetic collections as integrated, organized books, most especially those over which the poet took special interest in the exercise of editorial control. In French literature relatively few studies have centered on the concept of the poetry book.[9] Since the judgments many poets make concerning the arrangement and presentation of their poems is often a crucial component in the literary endeavor, contextual reading would offer more and better insights into the poet's work. Just as the position of individual elements within a poem determines the reader's perception of the work, so too does the placement of poems within a volume circumscribe the reading process. The principles of sequential integration may be quite distinct, such as clear logical or temporal sequencing from one poem to the next that furthers an argument or advances a narrative.[10] Others may be based on an easily identifiable extraliterary pattern of serial progression: alphabetical, calendrical, ritual, etc. The absence of clearly delineated schemes does not preclude integration. In many cases contextual links may be associative or dialectical—with superficial discontinuities—rather than logical or causal. In any case, textual cohesion ultimately relies on serial arrangement.[11]

Although readers and critics have traditionally viewed satire as a loosely organized, highly varied genre, numerous studies have demonstrated that Boileau's Latin predecessors were acutely aware of the structural design not only of isolated poems, but also of the books in which these poems were ordered. Like poets in other genres who arranged their poems in accordance with certain developmental principles, so too did Horace, Persius, and Juvenal.[12] Horace in particular has been the object of many, inevitably divergent, integrative studies that view his collections of individual satirical poems as unified entities. Classical scholars have contended, for example, that the group of ten poems making up Horace's first book of satires possesses a four-part structure that consists of three triads of *Satires 1–3, 4–6,* and *7–9,* with *Satire 10* weaving together and expanding the major themes of the preceding poems. Melding the motifs of freedom, friendship, personal development, literature, and power, Horace's first book apparently tells the story of the speaker's evolution from outsider to trusted member of Maecenas's inner circle.[13]

The fact that Boileau clearly saw the Roman satirists as literary forefathers advances my hypothesis that his *Satires* should be read as a totality, from start to finish, that each poem must be interpreted not merely as a discrete unit but also deciphered in light of its context within the body of the *Satires.* This task is inherently difficult, given the "disordered" nature of the genre, full of ambiguity, irony, apparent contradictions, tension between "serious" moral and philosophical statements of principle, and the comportment and inconsistencies of the speaker.

The historical tendency to see seemingly autonomous poems as lacking in unity and coherence, as merely amalgams of such elements as observations, portraits, personal anecdotes, opinions, and emotional pique, predisposes the reader to defer regarding the collected *Satires* as possessing any sort of structure, be it based on narrative progression, metaphorical convergences, belief patterns, or thematic association.

On the rare occasions when critics have provided readings of whole poems, each poem has for the most part been analyzed as a discrete work.[14] The relative inattention that the *Satires* have received as a potential poetic sequence can be seen in the study of Antoine Adam, who, in *Les Premières Satires de Boileau (I–IX),* examined all of *Satires I* through *IX,* including the *Discours au Roy,* in the order in which they were chronologically composed, which differs from the numerical order imposed on the poems by Boileau himself when they were published together.[15] Since they first appeared in 1666, the *Satires* have been arranged in numerical order. Adam asserts that the published order is "Purement arbitraire, il ne peut que gêner l'intelligence historique des *Satires.*"[16] This is true insofar as Adam's purpose is to explore the complex historical circumstances that stand as a backdrop to the composition of the satires.[17] Although Adam's procedure coincides with his intention, i.e., to elucidate extrinsic political, social, literary, and personal circumstances that may have affected the content of the poems, his study betrays the traditional historicist orientation of Boileau criticism.

The most obvious of serial markers, their numbers, must direct any integrative analysis of the *Satires.* To read the *Satires* in isolation from one another or in an order other than that of their numbers is to ignore Boileau's clear intention, which never wavered from the first authorized edition to the last published in his lifetime. We must assume that the author had excellent reasons for insisting on the order in which they have always appeared. Poetic time, not real time, imposes itself on our reading of the poems. The reading order of the poems creates its own dramatic time, and the earlier poems will affect our understanding of the later ones, and, in a more global perspective, the later ones may shed light on the developmental patterns and thematics uncovered in the prior poems. An imagined use and sense of time in the *Satires,* a progression—not a progress in the sense of advancement or refinement—specifies the speaker's own development over the fictional time scheme dictated by the reading of the poems. A multiplicity of dialogues in the *Satires*—within the speaker, between the speaker and his adversaries, with his allies, and ultimately with the reader—allows the reader to recognize and to comprehend the numerous features that make the speaker an individual. These traits include his fears, secret desires for happiness and for success, his impulses, peeves, hatreds, weaknesses, his view of humanity and the world, his relationship to the world and to his immediate environment, his attitude toward his profession, and the objects of his respect. As is the case with many sonnet sequences in which the persona is the main organizing and unifying principle, the speaker in the *Satires* stands at the focal point of numerous thematic departures.

Chapter One

The *Discours au Roy*

Conflicted Beginnings

A sequential reading of the *Satires* compels us to give special consideration to the collection's initial poem, the *Discours au Roy*. Its crucial opening position generates and determines the reader's expectations concerning the body of poems that follow. After placing the poem between *Satires V* and *VI* in the first authorized 1666 edition, Boileau set the work in its leading position in the second printing of his *œuvres* published the following year. Although evidence indicates that Boileau completed the *Discours au Roy* after *Satires I, II, IV, V, VI,* and *VII,* the author clearly felt that the poem's subject and themes justified the decision to place the work in its definitive introductory position. As Georges Ascoli (11) points out, Mathurin Régnier's 1608 edition of his *Satires* provided the young poet with a well-known precedent for this arrangement.[1]

In this poem Boileau confronts a seemingly intractable problem for the satirist writing in the age of Louis XIV: How can the satirist, whose stock in trade is irony and sarcastic mockery of pomposity, devise a poem whose generic demands include the solemn invocation of a venerated object?[2] Boileau's solution is to create a generic hybrid, a work that traces a middle course between the genres of panegyric and satire. On the metaphorical and thematic levels, dichotomous images and themes of sight/blindness, youth/age, truth/falsehood, genuineness/deceit, enduring renown / ephemeral notoriety, singular distinction / common insignificance, and a temporal perspective encompassing the past, present, and future recur throughout the *Discours au Roy*. These patterns reinforce Boileau's aesthetic juggling act, the generic intermingling of encomium and satire.[3]

The conflict between *laudatio* and *vituperatio* plays a key role in the arguments that contend within the speaker's psyche in the course of the *Satires*. The *Discours au Roy* begins as a conventional panegyric. Its opening lines intone the customary divine qualities of the precocious monarch, who miraculously combines youth, military prowess, and wisdom:

> Jeune et vaillant Heros, dont la haute sagesse
> N'est point le fruit tardif d'une lente vieillesse,
> Et qui seul, sans Ministre, à l'exemple des Dieux,
> Soûtiens tout par Toi-mesme, et vois tout par Tes yeux.

More importantly, the King, who rules ". . . sans Ministre" (v. 3),[4] displays singular autonomy in the exercise of his power and judgment.[5] Since panegyric often alludes to the all-seeing and all-sustaining qualities of its object,[6] Louis's godlike mastery of his domain accordingly prompts implicit comparison in v. 4 to a pair of heroic mythological deities, Atlas and Argos. The former, whose slightest stumble would plunge the world back into primeval chaos, evokes incredible strength, while the latter conjures up a panorama of eponymous characters who embody the themes of perpetual vision, intrepid adventure, and unparalleled craftsmanship.[7]

While the familiar pronoun intensifies the prayerlike invocational tone of the first four verses, it also subtly contributes to a tendency toward personal affinity between speaker and addressee that, although at first glance seeming to verge on impudence, takes on greater resonance as the poem progresses. Attributes belonging to the King—relative youth, energetic self-confidence, and, above all, supreme independence—might also be ascribed to the speaker as he gradually reveals himself in the course of the poem's development.[8] Despite the "stile pompeux" (v. 21) of the conventional panegyric with which the poem opens, the speaker will strive to create a bond, however far-fetched, if he remained solely within the artificial confines of the genre, between himself and the King. Stemming from the opposing genres in which the speaker finds himself embroiled in this ostensible poem of praise, this clash of means and ends persists to the conclusion.[9] The poem thus becomes as much a self-justification as an official work intended to glorify and thus flatter Louis XIV.

The speaker must first explain his erstwhile reluctance to extol the King. In an admission that will become a leitmotif in succeeding satires, the speaker declares his ineptitude in the genre of panegyric.[10] Thus, from the opening lines of the collection's introductory poem, the speaker launches the themes of potential silence, unabashed self-knowledge, and the consequent awareness of personal limitations, tempered by an assortment of strong and consistently held beliefs. First, the speaker must entreat his master not to construe his "humble silence" (v. 6) as disrespect: quite the contrary is the case. More precisely, because of this perceived deficiency, his profound veneration for the King has prevented the speaker from singing his praises. The image of the "cœur vainement suspendu" (v. 7), lacking a firm *point d'attache*, underscores the notion that the speaker, on the other hand, clings to strongly held convictions and, more importantly, never hesitates to express them, provided that the means are at his command. Like the unshakable Louis, who furnishes a sturdy base of support for his kingdom (v. 4), the speaker associates himself with stability and constancy (vv. 7–8). The reciprocal relationship suggested by the verb *offrir* in vv. 8 and 11 further advances the convergence of speaker and addressee in this poem. The King's magnanimous self-offering to his subjects in turn prompts the speaker to proffer a panegyric decidedly unlike the standard poem of praise. The speaker's persistent self-disclosure—in fact another kind of self-offering—partly overshadows the true object of the poem and tends to subvert the genre of panegyric.

Despite his aversion to generic bombast, the speaker manages to extol Louis's grandeur while simultaneously maintaining the network of analogies between himself and his addressee. Just as the King has the power to see and to penetrate all through his own eyes (v. 4), the speaker rejects the temptation to "blind" himself (v. 13) to his own aesthetic liabilities and imprudently pursue a genre ill-suited to his muse. The speaker's compunction—seen in his fear that his "touch" would wither Louis's "lauriers" (v. 12) and his well-advised unwillingness to "soar" beyond his range (v. 14)—wisely avoids the recklessness of two mythological exemplars of foolish presumption evoked by Boileau's images, Midas and Icarus.[11] Meticulous self-cognizance thus deters the speaker from repeating the disastrous fate of these mythic archetypes, a quality sadly missing among the legion of daring "Mortels" (v. 15) who value personal financial advantage above legitimate artistic concerns. The presence of these contemptible and willfully ignorant parasites (especially in their reckless disregard of the lessons to be gleaned from the Midas and Icarus legends) challenges the validity of panegyric, a genre whose *raison d'être*, above all else, naively presupposes the sincerity of an author untainted by self-interest. In his detachment from this throng of mercenaries, the unique speaker further accentuates his identification with the equally singular King.[12]

From the outset the speaker endeavors to stake out for himself poetic territory that his rivals have failed even to recognize, much less occupy. Boileau has composed an unorthodox panegyric that bypasses—without neglecting it altogether—the conventional praise lavished on the addressee in order to instruct Louis on quite delicate matters. Realizing that yet another pointless *éloge* would merely bore the vigorous young King (vv. 19–20), the speaker elevates him in terms whose grandiloquence masks an intent to establish a tacit empathy between King and subject. Despite the face-value absurdity of the proposition, his attempts to create a sense of affiliation, to authenticate his credentials as a solitary, impartial observer who in reality has much in common with the young King, allow him to address a less skeptical reader.

Proceeding inductively in pursuit of his didactic objectives, the speaker in vv. 21–48 portrays two succinct examples of the poetical rabble pestering His Majesty. Referring in turn to François Charpentier and Jean Chapelain, vv. 21–28 target specific deficiencies, which we can summarize as witless incoherence. To use the eclogue as a vehicle for panegyric ("L'Un en stilc pompeux habillant une eglogue" [v. 21]) exposes not only abysmal taste, but also complete neglect of generic parameters, since the popular eclogue depicted amorous shepherds, demanded a middle style, and aimed to create a sense of ideal peace and tranquillity in its reader![13] This melding of incompatible poetic modes accompanies gross betrayal of the prime objective of elegy, i.e., to lionize its addressee. The ludicrous commixture of praise for the King with the poet's *autolouange* receives special emphasis in v. 24, in which the oxymoronic combination "Fat"/"Heros" is placed in prominent rhythmic positions. Whereas the composer of laughable eclogues fails to comprehend the value of generic codes, the second poet lacks the wit to produce meaningful rhymes. Generating such insipid juxtapositions as "pareil"/"Soleil," which the speaker sarcastically parodies in vv. 27–28 ("Grand et nouvel effort d'un esprit sans pareil! / Dans la fin d'un sonnet Te compare au Soleil"), his endless revisions result in the most banal of *pointes*. In their foolish audacity, ignorance, inflated *amour-propre*, dearth of good taste, and ultimate failure, the two would-be poets share important traits with the mythic Icarus and Midas, from whom the speaker disassociated himself in vv. 11–14.

The speaker's didactic purpose intensifies at v. 29. As an informative intercessor between his primary reader and the mysteries of Parnassus, a role he assumes by virtue of his stance as a poet steeped in his craft (vv. 9–20), the speaker divulges the "true" status of these two frauds "Sur le haut Helicon" (v. 29). Scorned and rejected by the Muses, of whom the most eminent is Calliope, muse of epic poetry and of eloquence, as well as by Pegasus, the poetic *poseurs* have the temerity to lie to the King by misrepresenting their prestige in Apollo's court (vv. 34–43). The speaker subtly suggests that this false promise (v. 34)—no less than a brazen act of lèse-majesté—would potentially make the King himself an object of ridicule and even contempt among the gods of poetry! Fortunately, Louis's intrinsic luster, which requires no extraneous assistance to illuminate the earth, will avert such an appalling eventuality. The speaker thus exposes the self-serving function and the bogus claims of the treacherous versifiers who regularly exalt the King. In reversing the poets' pretense that their genius will assure the King's immortality, the speaker, naturally, seizes the opportunity to celebrate Louis's self-sustaining grandeur.

In v. 49 the speaker changes his tactics. Anticipating charges of unfairness and brazen temerity ("ma plume injuste et temeraire"), he takes care to specify that celebrating the King in verse remains a noble undertaking. Although the divine Sun King obviously needs no wretched scribblers (e.g., Charpentier and Chapelain) to proclaim his brilliance, there exist in the realm poetic talents worthy of the King ("Parmi les Pelletiers on conte des Corneilles" [v. 54]). Among these talents, of course, stands the speaker. His healthy dose of fair-mindedness supplies a modicum of balance to a discourse in which he must constantly consider the consequences of obsessive rancor or, at the opposite end of the scale, extravagant goodwill. Describing an intuitive reflex that will receive further development in the course of this poem and in the other *Satires* as well, he reveals his antipathy toward inane writers. He posits a kind of equilibrium of merit between poet and patron that is essential for effective panegyric ("Pour chanter un Auguste, il faut estre un Virgile" [v. 58]). Modeled upon the example of the immortal Alexander, who forbade anyone other than the incomparable Apelles to paint his portrait,[14] the speaker's implied advice creates a possible analogy between Louis and the ancient conqueror, thus praising the King while avoiding the blatant groveling of direct comparison. The speaker's discreet advice to the King communicates a harsh message: that he repudiate the vile poetry of traitors and imitate Alexander, thus accomplishing no less than the safeguarding of his eternal renown.

Such frankness must rest on the speaker's stated reverence for the truth as he perceives it and must further rely on reinforcing the crucial points of affinity, suggested earlier, between subject and object. Beginning at v. 63, he attenuates the implicitly professed expertise of vv. 21–48, again alleging his own youth (birth dates: Louis, Sept. 5, 1638; Boileau, Nov. 1, 1636). In v. 66 the emphasis placed on the joy to be gained in his poetic apprenticeship adumbrates the fundamental theme of pleasure from the writing process that the speaker finds essential and mentions often in the subsequent satires. His modest admission of inexperience (Louis may be equally inexperienced, but the speaker dare not say so!) counterbalances another bold analogy with the young King in vv. 67–70:

> Et tandis que Ton bras des peuples redouté,
> Va, la foudre à la main, rétablir l'équité,
> Et retient les Méchans par la peur des supplices:
> Moi, la plume à la main, je gourmande les vices.

Syntactic parallelism ("Va, la foudre à la main . . ." / "Moi, la plume à la main . . .") implies that both are young heroes who fight for "l'équité" (v. 68) and against "les vices" (v. 70). While the disparity of the comparison (weapon: "foudre"/"plume"; target: "peuples" / "moindres sujets" (v. 66), with a possible pun on "sujets") hints at outright burlesque, the speaker's serious tone of self-disclosure rather evokes his own desire for truth and heartfelt sincerity in stark contrast to the Charpentiers, Chapelains, and Pelletiers, who unjustly have the King's ear: "Et gardant pour moi-mesme une juste rigueur, / Je confie au papier les secrets de mon cœur" (vv. 71–72).[15]

Boileau's peculiar panegyric to Louis begins to stray farther from its "proper" subject as the speaker moves from underlining affinities with his addressee to a more developed description and concomitant apology of his work. The bee metaphor in vv. 74–76 directs attention to the single-minded behavior of (stinging) bee and speaker, yet the latter draws sustenance from the "sottises du temps" (v. 76) and transforms this into something quite opposite from the bee's sweet "miel." The bitter "fiel" that he produces from his harvest of "sottises" all around him materializes as naturally and instinctively as the bee's honey. Also like the bee, the speaker flits from *sottise* to *sottise*, directed solely by the inscrutable dictates of his muse (vv. 77–78).[16] The same freedom applies to his barbed pen during composition: "Et, sans gesner ma plume en ce libre métier, / Je la laisse au hazard courir sur le papier" (vv. 79–80). Although the traditional concept of satire as an autonomous, an unfettered, free-form genre seems to deviate from the now defunct, received notion of Boileau's classicism as expressed in the *Art poétique*, the theme returns again and again in his work.[17] Inasmuch as we can interpret the *Discours au Roy* as a prolegomenon to the subsequent satires, it is fitting that he emphasize this prime attribute of satire in this opening poem.

The liberty of the speaker's "veine" (v. 77) as to subject extends as well to his muse's compulsion to identify—to *name*—the precise source of his "fiel" (v. 76). The speaker introduces the frequent theme of widespread fear generated by the satirist, perhaps courageous, perhaps foolish, who peels off layers of deceit to expose the truth beneath. Just as the speaker has demonstrated with his excoriation of the pair of impostors who parade their pretend poetry before the King, he will forever strive to unearth truth, however deeply it may be buried. As suggested by his tendency to name names referred to in v. 82, Boileau's choice technique of providing a particular example here produces a most famous one: Molière's *Tartuffe* and the virulent reaction of the *parti dévot* when it premiered in 1664.

Putting aside Boileau's unfailing critical instincts in naming a now legendary case of hypocrisy exposed, the adversaries of truth attack in support of secular and spiritual values that underpin the monarchy itself ("C'est offenser les loix, c'est s'attaquer aux Cieux" [v. 96]). Not unlike Charpentier and Chapelain, these "Bigots" (v. 94) exploit the King's most cherished aspirations—religious and civil justice in this case—to pursue selfish, even treasonous, ends. In sum, Molière and Louis have common enemies who will stop at nothing to subjugate their anathema, Truth.[18] The speaker thus invokes a kind of triumvirate of (un)equals, all steadfast champions of honor, integrity, and veracity: Louis, Molière, and Boileau.

At v. 103 ("Mais pourquoi sur ce point sans raison m'écarter?"), the speaker provides critical self-analysis pertaining to the developmental structure of the poem. Long condemned as a failure at supplying smooth transitions in his work, Boileau oftentimes draws the reader's attention to these apparent internal inconsistencies by commenting on them. The "digression" on religious hypocrisy and Molière's conflict with it does not, however, qualify as such, for the reasons above proposed. Moreover, v. 103 seems superfluous in view of vv. 77–80, which acknowledge and justify the speaker's tendency to wander. The speaker's self-incrimination coincides with his protest of incompetence in v. 104 ("GRAND ROI, c'est mon defaut, je ne sçaurois flatter"), echoing v. 9 ("Mais je sçais peu loüer . . ."). In reality of course, his inability to flatter the King flatters the speaker, since it separates him from the mob of sycophants for whom insincerity is a way of life. Clearly, the speaker's unalloyed devotion to Truth makes him the ideal panegyrist, provided that his subject is truly laudable! In fact, Louis must be told that neither riches, renown, legal constraints, nor physical force could coerce plaudits from the speaker's compulsively sincere pen.

Verses 103–14 prepare that portion of the poem, vv. 115–30, that belies the speaker's professed incompetence in elegy. Given his insistence on his compulsive candor, these lines emerge not as the overt flattery that they appear to be, but rather as objective statements of fact made by an open-eyed observer ("Mais lorsque je Te voi . . ." [v. 115]; "Quand je voi . . ." [v. 119; cf. also v. 13]). They are a concrete example of the speaker's spontaneous muse in full flight, who "Nomme tout par son nom, et ne sçauroit rien taire" (v. 82). Just as the speaker has propounded the concept of the ideal model among a host of lesser examples by offering himself as the paragon of panegyrists lost in a multitude of poetic windbags, the King is presented in like terms: Louis can "Faire honte à ces Rois, que le travail étonne, / Et qui sont accablez du faix de leur Couronne" (vv. 117–18). A leitmotif in the *Satires*, the basic notion of quantity versus quality plays a significant role in this introductory poem. The image of ponderous weight associated with lesser kings reinforces Louis's almost ethereal ease in extending his "haute sagesse" (v. 1) over the planet: at home (v. 120), abroad (v. 121), at sea (v. 122), and into the farthest reaches of the globe (v. 128).

A portent of Raison's recurring intervention in subsequent *Satires*, the speaker's glorious voyage of praise, piloted by his impetuous muse, is suddenly halted in v. 131. The clash between panegyric and satire, antithetical genres which nonetheless both rely for ultimate success on the speaker's sincerity as perceived by the reader, explains Raison's brusque intercession. The essential problem centers on the manner in which the speaker's candor can be communicated to the reader. Although the fearful speaker asserts his lack of "strength" and hastily lets fall the generic burden that he has impulsively taken on (vv. 134–36), he realizes that continued indulgence in the "stile pompeux" that he had ridiculed in the beginning of the poem makes him vulnerable to the same charges of venal hypocrisy, not to mention artistic ineptitude, that he had flung at others. In this sense the poem becomes an indictment of the genre of panegyric as commonly practiced and the rhetoric peculiar to it.[19] Fraudulent panegyrists such as Charpentier and Chapelain have contributed in no small way to this generic depreciation. The speaker's objective—to convince his addressee that his words are true and honest—is unattainable if he remains within the tattered panegyric genre. Raison therefore arrives to "rescue" him (v. 131) from his predicament.

Even more so than panegyric, the success of satire depends on the reader's faith that the satirist, more properly the poetic persona, speaks from innermost conviction. Like any satirist, Boileau creates this effect of sincerity not only through his explicit claims but also by way of satire's informal tone, apparent spontaneity, casual structure, comic devices, and general irreverence, all of which are present in the poem's conclusion. The shifts from the formalized rhetoric of vv. 119–28 to the confiding language of vv. 131–36 and the comic flourish with which the piece closes in vv. 137–40 encapsulate the generic modulation at the heart of the poem's structure.[20] The speaker's epic journey "Aux lieux où le Soleil le [l'or] forme en se levant" (v. 128) cannot "passer plus loin" (v. 137), because a tempest has forced the now burlesque, cowardly speaker to jump ship and swim for his life! And what of his pilotless poetic vessel?[21]

If the writer of panegyric "invites his reader to gaze with him at something else," Boileau's *Discours au Roy* actually invites the reader to gaze at his speaker, who directs more attention to his own traits than to those of his celebrated addressee. This project of self-disclosure is crucial in regard to the thematic development of the subsequent *Satires*. The speaker's speech "au Roy" portrays a writer of satire whose youth not unexpectedly accompanies a powerful sense of independence. Fearless in freely expressing his strong opinions on the art of poetry, this young poet takes pride in his adherence to truth and to his own honesty in declaring that truth as he sees it. Clearly, this self-portrait also reveals a solid foundation of self-knowledge. Among the voices within him, self-doubt as to his own talent often makes itself heard above the other, more confident inflections. Typical among youth, the all-important power of example—whether positive or negative—will persist as an instrumental source of authority in the ensuing *Satires*.

Chapter Two

Two Poetic Paradigms

While in the *Discours au Roy* the speaker suggested a network of flattering analogies between himself and the ostensible object of the poem, *Satire I* shifts to a different kind of character altogether, the poetic failure Damon. Syntactic parallelism in vv. 1–4 of each poem reinforces the dialectical relationship between Louis and Damon. This incongruous pair becomes a threesome if we look forward to vv. 1–4 of *Satire II,* where an identical syntactical scheme introduces Molière.[1] This disparate trio possesses attributes that make each of the men remarkable individuals in themselves, yet their real significance lies in what they represent for the speaker. Described in the *Discours au Roy,* his status as a young and relatively inexperienced, yet independent and tough-minded, poet affects how each may be interpreted. By providing positive or negative examples, each figure represents influential values that motivate the speaker's beliefs and attitudes concerning his vocation, the world around him, and his own self-image. As the powerful potential *mécène,* the King contrasts sharply with the failed poet Damon; both, however, allow the speaker to delve further into his own self-awareness, knowledge that will evolve and gradually unfold as the *Satires* progress. Damon's speech contains much that the speaker of the *Discours au Roy,* whose role is limited to vv. 1–20 in *Satire I,* would accept as true. The fact that the embittered old poet verbalizes this denunciation allows his presenter to promote some of his own views while maintaining at the very least a pretense of objectivity, thus shielding himself from the official dangers that such an attitude would create for the young poet of the *Discours au Roy.*

The poem designated as the first *Satire* is in fact Boileau's earliest, supposedly begun when he was nineteen or twenty years of age (Escal, in her ed. of Boileau's *Œuvres complètes* 866; Ascoli 21). It depicts the withdrawal of a middle-aged, disgruntled, and apparently old-fashioned poet, in effect a *raté,* from a great European capital, renowned center of culture and learning. Notwithstanding Mascarille's *bon mot* in *Les Précieuses ridicules*—"hors de Paris, il n'y a point de salut pour les honnêtes gens!" (Molière, scene ix)—the disappointed Damon views Paris as an overwhelming obstacle to his own salvation. His avowed animosity for Paris, its institutions, and its people prevails over the generally accepted notion that the poetic enterprise demands the social ferment that a large metropolis alone can offer. Commenting on Juvenal's third satire, Matthew Hodgart shares this view: "Most writers, after all, have lived in cities for part of their lives: even if they prefer to live in the country, their patrons and public are in the capital cities, which are the centers of political and cultural life, and where most interesting events take place" (Hodgart 135).[2] Among the French poets who sing the praises of Paris as capital of the arts and the good life is Boileau's antithesis, Antoine-Girard de Saint-Amant, who in "Les Cabarets" exhorts his friend Faret to *return* to the earthly paradise that he sees in Paris.[3] Damon's desire for flight is rooted, however, in the simple notion that he can no longer tolerate the corruption that he sees in the city.[4] In Paris, real poetry is impossible. In becoming a *persona non grata,* the experienced poet's litany of grievances makes it obvious that his work is *passé,* unappreciated, and scorned, according to Damon, by an ignorant and degenerate public.

Moral overtones provide counterpoint to the purely pragmatic reasons for Damon's withdrawal. Indeed, Damon's retreat from the capital takes on a spiritual cast: He assumes the identity of the devout penitent who retires from the temporal realm of those who have elected to pursue worldly gain at the expense of the divine. In doing so he is emulating many another Counter-Reformation sinner, in French life as well as in literature, who forsook the *monde* for the *désert* to find oneness with God. This aspiration for the immutable underscores the transience of all that Damon is escaping. Once a popular figure in the literary world, Damon has experienced firsthand the ups and downs of Fortune's wheel.

Boileau's immediate inspiration for *Satire I* is Juvenal's third satire.[5] Like Boileau's poem, its first twenty verses serve as a preamble to the monologue of the virulently unhappy, middle-aged Umbricius, who rails against the dishonesty, immorality, injustice, discomforts, and dangers of Rome. Explicit in his diatribe is a set of contrasts between city and country, rich and poor, foreigner and native, and flattery and sincerity. His own code of honor renders him powerless in a city where integrity is the shortest route to poverty.[6] Unlike in the French poem, in Juvenal the introducer commends his friend Umbricius's disdainful rejection of Rome. As in the French poem, however, the addressee stays behind despite this agreement. Boileau's narrator limits his introduction to a relatively impartial description of Damon's past and present circumstances, emphasizing his current extreme destitution, the constant threat of the justice reserved for debtors, and his dominant emotion, anger. Also, in Juvenal, Umbricius is not explicitly identified as a poet, whereas the introducer in Boileau's piece presents Damon as an author from the opening hemistich.

Long a leitmotif in satiric poetry,[7] Damon's poverty receives close attention in vv. 1–20. The presenter immediately establishes contrast between the poet's productive and presumably prosperous past, during which time his work met wide acceptance (". . . dont la Muse fertile / Amusa si long-temps, et la Cour et la Ville" [vv. 1–2]), and his impecunious and desiccated present ("Et de qui le corps sec, et la mine affamée, / N'en sont pas mieux refaits pour tant de renommée" [vv. 5–6]). Although he was a "grand Auteur" (we should not discount the irony inherent in the adjective),[8] Damon's function was confined merely to the amusement of his public (note the stressed position of "Amusa" in v. 2): the contemporary literary corollary to *plaire,* i.e., *instruire,* is omitted. This is appropriate, given the unenlightened, morally obtuse Parisian audience denounced in his peroration. Is the therefore ineffectual Damon at least partially to blame for the intellectual and ethical wasteland that he wishes to leave behind in Paris? Erstwhile creative abundance having degenerated into material as well as mental indigence, Damon has in effect become a zero, a naked nonentity: "Sans habits, sans argent, ne sçachant plus que faire, / Vient de s'enfuir chargé de sa seule misere" (vv. 9–10). Damon's figurative nudity denotes his disconnection from the society that his very nakedness obliges him to flee. Numerous biblical passages relate exposure of the body to loss of grace, to material and spiritual degradation. A social pariah, Damon must escape from the origins of this shame: he yearns not only for physical but also for spiritual renewal.

The poet's principal and most immediate nemesis is a system of justice represented by its agents ("des Sergens, des Clercs" [v. 11]), which will either deprive him of liberty "le reste de sa vie" (v. 14) or confer a "bonnet vert"—a sign of opprobrium worn by those who have agreed to cede all worldly possessions to their creditors ("salutaire" [v. 15], because it "saves" the debtor from prison). Ironically, the *bonnet vert* has supplanted his—likewise green—crown of drooping laurel, obvious symbol of his bygone eminence. Once wreathed in a plant redolent of poetic glory and seemingly immortal renown, Damon now is threatened with a "crown" of contrary significance. Moreover, the *bonnet vert* emerges as "salutaire" inasmuch as its menace has led Damon to seek refuge from the accursed city and will lead him to his eventual *salut.* Replacing the natural laurel leaves, the green bonnet, an item of human construction, compels the passé poet to seek out the natural sanctuary afforded by "quelque antre ou quelque roche" (v. 25). As in Juvenal's satire, contrast between corrupt city and untainted country plays a role in Boileau's piece, yet Damon's quest transcends this traditional dichotomy.

The narrator's concluding words provide clues to a thematic feature of the poem necessarily absent in Juvenal: the poet's search for his soul's renewal and his ultimate salvation. Described as a "Penitent sur la fin d'un Carême" (v. 18), Damon displays not only fury but a "burning" passion (". . . le feu dans les yeux" [v. 19]) not for vengeance on a city that he sees as the root of damnation, but rather for spiritual retreat and purification far from the abyss. His ragged clothes, gaunt look, and fiery eyes identify him as the pious and ascetic Christian—a former sinner who has seen the light—railing against the iniquity of the world. Damon's farewell harangue opens on the underlying opposition of virtuous past vs. vice-ridden present. Like the allegorical "Vertu" lamented in v. 24 (". . . ici la Vertu n'a ni feu ni lieu"), the poet finds himself without essential material needs. His alternative is to find sanctuary in "quelque antre ou quelque roche" (v. 25), an undertaking recalling the lives of numerous saints in the Catholic tradition.[9]

A conventional symbol for the everlasting in contrast to the transitory, the solid rock "antre" stands as a remote, solitary haven in geographical as well as temporal terms. A pun on "temps" in v. 28 ("Mettons-nous à l'abri des injures du temps") plays comically on the dual nature of Damon's quest: material succor, but especially spiritual cleansing outside the mere physical passage of time itself. Damon seeks an ideal *locus amoenus* where time stands still, where, for example, a poet's good reputation might remain impervious to passing public fancies: ". . . en ce Lieu jadis aux Muses si commode, / Le mérite et l'esprit ne sont plus à la mode" (vv. 21–22). The fact that Damon is not at an advanced age, i.e., near to death's door, heightens the earnestness of his pilgrimage far from Paris; not for him the hasty repentance of those for whom death is near. In any event, Damon's desperate impoverishment imposes his irrevocable decision to withdraw from the "world": "C'est là dans mon malheur le seul conseil à suivre" (v. 33), since in Paris the poet "s'y voit maudit de Dieu" (v. 23). Hesitation can only assure damnation.

In the poem's subsequent section, Damon concentrates on those who, quite unlike himself, flourish in the moral filth of Paris. His first case in point is George, whose ill-gotten gains have miraculously transformed him from a humble lackey to a not-so-blue-blooded marquis. Introduced as was George by the concessive subjunctive ("Que Jaquin vive ici" [v. 37; rhymes with *faquin!*]), the second example ironically illustrates a conniving financier who, quite unlike the hapless Damon, has enriched himself through his "writings." The celebrated Jaquin's sophisticated understanding of the alphabet (". . . ses revenus écrits par alphabet" [v. 39]) has handsomely rewarded his labors! The prolific Jaquin's "Calepin complet," denoting a heavy tome—a *calepin* being in seventeenth-century usage a thick dictionary—ironically accentuates his authorial accomplishments.

The unscrupulous Jaquin's prosperity is in direct opposition to the speaker's poverty, a patent contrast reinforced by the stark return to self-analysis in v. 42: "Mais moi, vivre à Paris: Eh, qu'y voudrois-je faire?"[10] Damon's invective expands on his scathing portrayal of the honest writer's lot in Paris. Totally incapable of what he would call outright lying, whether it be exaggerated praise in honor of the highest bidder or insincere love sonnets written to satisfy a rich patron's appetite for seduction, Damon professes his incompatibility with current Parisian mores. The poet's uncompromising Alceste-like stance further underlines the perceived gap between past and present city life. Indeed, given Damon's antiurban bias, his prideful insistence on rustic origins and simplicity, and his inability to use oblique language ("Je ne puis rien nommer, si ce n'est par son nom" [v. 51]: a peculiar source of pride for a poet!), the reader may ask how this singular poet could possibly have entertained "et la Cour et la Ville" for so long! Damon's present elevated, even sacred, view of his poetic art (see esp. v. 48, where he suggests an analogy between incense, redolent of the divine, and his own verses) bolsters his resolve to leave a place that robs him of his soul ("Ainsi qu'un corps sans ame" [v. 56]).

The intervention of a third party in v. 57, a voice ("dira-t-on") challenging the "vertu sauvage" of the disgruntled poet, appears to prefigure Molière's urbane Philinte, preaching compromise with a society that will adhere to its own rules regardless of the upright individual's indignation and disapproval. This bodiless articulation of moral concession and adaptation to "reality" in vv. 57–64 initiates a dialogical process that underlines the essentially relative nature of such opposing philosophical positions. The continuing silence of the poet's introducer of vv. 1–20 emphasizes his objectivity in this dispute. This reluctance to intercede emphasizes his own neutrality in a debate focusing on issues central to the life of the artist in society. The interlocutor would agree with the poet that times have indeed changed (". . . cette vertu sauvage, / Qui court à l'hospital, et n'est *plus* en usage?" [vv. 57–58; my emphasis]), but contends that the clever author can overcome the disgrace and injustices that Damon so vehemently deplores. The third party's apparent disdain for the man of letters ("un Pédant" [v. 64]) provokes Damon's tirade in vv. 65–80 condemning a world in which blind and capricious Fortune holds sway over stolid but ineffectual Virtue, recalling his comments on *la Vertu* in v. 24. As in prior verses, recourse to example bolsters Damon's case that Fortune's wheel will unfailingly topple Virtue's rightful supremacy. Heaven itself cannot punish the swindling financier who, now temporarily exiled from the metropolis, will recover from this setback and return in triumph, enriched by thievery (v. 75). He contrasts sharply with Damon who, like the financier, flees the capital, but who will never come back, and if so, certainly not crowned with success. In vv. 77–80 another example, Guillaume Colletet, corroborates Damon's point that the poet is doomed to starvation in a merciless city.

The poem's ensuing section beginning at v. 81 shifts the locus of the discourse from the *ville* to the *cour,* thus following the initial pattern suggested in v. 2. The fate of the sincere poet at court, that ultimate arbiter of taste, is at least as cruel as in the city, since he must play by the same debased rules. Although the speaker takes care not to implicate the King himself in his general condemnation of the situation at court, his accusations echo his previous charges.

The vast throng of supplicants who petition the court thwart the just King's best attempts to assist impoverished writers. In vv. 91–92 the image of predatory poets rushing headlong to snatch at the King's outstretched hand ("Qui, dés que sa main s'ouvre, y courent les premiers, / Et ravissent un bien qu'on devoit aux derniers") invokes Christ's admonition that in the kingdom of heaven the last will be first and the first last (Matt. 19.23–30; Mark 10.23–31). In the biblical passage, the rich man's inevitable exclusion from paradise[11] substantiates Damon's quest for spiritual purification and his moral denunciation of the city and the court. Damon's proud refusal to participate in this degrading struggle for royal stipends contrasts with the humiliations willingly accepted and thus condoned by the mass ("troupe lâche et sterile" [v. 93]) of obsequious poets importuning the King.

From this confused mob the speaker selects a single example, the unfortunate Saint-Amant (vv. 97–112). Despite the prevailing opinion that Boileau's animus found Antoine-Girard de Saint-Amant a particularly juicy target, Damon notes that this Saint-Amant's poverty-induced death from fever was due to the court's rejection of his work, not, explicitly, to the abject quality of his work. This example is a warning to writers who naively believe that good taste will triumph and that exceptional poetry will be recognized and duly rewarded at court. As in the city, current fashion is to despise and to ostracize even the finest of poets. The speaker, perhaps self-servingly, declares that talent has absolutely nothing to do with courtly approbation. Given the horrifying circumstances of Saint-Amant's fate and his conviction that he is now traveling the same road, Damon (and the presenter) must consider whether another profession might offer better opportunity for a fruitful life.

Damon's brief reflections on a career change to the law must be rejected out of hand, especially in view of the most immediate reason for his flight from Paris, escape from a system of justice that pursues and severely punishes debtors (vv. 11–16). The ridiculous analogy between the sublime Apollo and the grotesque Bartole (v. 114), combined with a reference to the renowned "authors" of the bar in v. 115, Loüet and Brodeau, reinforces the burlesque correspondence established between the worlds of the law and of letters. Furthermore, the poet's indictment of this "païs barbare" (v. 118) employs literary commonplaces, evoking the myth of the Minotaur tracking down and devouring "Innocence" (v. 119) in his "Dédale" (v. 120), and parallels the sorry state of affairs among poets, who presumably propagate reams of worthless paper, just as the law's labyrinthine rules and procedures ("les formes" [v. 122]) create mounds of equally worthless paper.

Damon's revulsion at the very thought of living off the law provides impetus for his concluding blast in vv. 137–44, in which he deftly summarizes his grievances against Paris and its denizens. That prime emotional motivation for the satirical poet, pure anger (cf. vv. 19–20), propels this writer's invective to the point where he must pause for breath (v. 136), emphasizing the oral modality of his discourse. Damon's contention that the infuriating moral depravity that he sees everywhere around him is ample inspiration for the writer of satire appears to confute his fundamental enterprise, i.e., to forsake this fertile source of poetry. Despite Damon's financial distress and moral indignation, his wish for liberation, we must remember, stems from his fear of damnation in this most diabolical of cities. Although Parisian society not unexpectedly emerges as an inexhaustible fount of inspiration for the poet of satire, Damon's conviction that his salvation hangs in the balance overrides mere artistic considerations.

Damon asserts that the writer with a satirical bent need only observe what is manifest everywhere around him (vv. 132–36), react in righteous anger (vv. 137–40), and channel that outrage to the written page, "pour écrire avec grace" (v. 141). Spurred on by choler rather than by *fureur,* the satirist need not scale Parnassian heights in his quest for inspiration and consequent glory. The sudden intervention, however, of "quelqu'un" in v. 145 exposes the fundamental predicament of the literary satirist: others, whether targeted in his work or not, object that satire is not a legitimate literary genre. The preacher, from the moral eminence of his *chaire,* has the prerogative to fulminate against the foibles of the age, but not a genuine poet! Thus the subject turns to literature in general and to the legitimacy of satire.

Unwilling to debate the relative merits of satire as a literary genre, Damon reverts to the moral stance displayed at the beginning of his tirade. Impervious to the mortal danger that he has put himself in by accepting the present state of affairs in Paris, the *libertin* critic nonetheless is in peril of forfeiting his very soul unless he acknowledges the satirist's moral authority. This sudden shift to the religious tends to identify satire as ultimately the most worthwhile of genres. He who stays and remains unheedful of the truth that satire teaches must be prepared to accept the horrendous consequences. His flight carries with it a dire warning to those who stay.

What then of the presenter? In his opening remarks much less judgmental than Damon, he remains in Paris, perhaps to profit, perhaps not, from Damon's angry lesson. Although unintended, an essential component of this sermon is the principle that he who abandons Paris (despite spiritual advantages) consigns himself to poetic (especially satiric) nullity. When juxtaposed to Damon's fury, the presenter's very objectivity suggests at the least his neutrality toward the older poet's intentions. While Damon's reflections on the debasement of a Paris that is in his mind no longer "Paris" contain invaluable and entertaining insights, his decision does not necessarily extend to others. The presenter's objectivity suggests that he must suspend judgment as to Paris's Sodom-like wickedness as described in Damon's tirade. The fate of the *dépassé* older poet may eventually be that of the younger observer, yet he must remain to struggle and to create in the only setting where such creation is possible, the very core of all that the satirist disdains and thereby strives to obliterate. The example of Damon may serve as a cautionary tale to the young poet, perhaps foreshadowing his own unhappy future.[12] The following poem, however, provides an opposing—ideal—image, which the speaker aspires to emulate.

His fourth *Satire* in order of composition, according to Boileau's commentator Pierre Le Verrier (Ascoli 45), *Satire II* immediately provokes possible comparison and contrast to *Satire I.* Syntactic parallelism in vv. 1–2 of both poems suggests potent analogies between the insolvent poetic *raté* Damon, who was once "ce grand Auteur," and Molière, the "Rare et fameux Esprit" who composes with such amazing facility. Each author exhibits—or at least exhibited, in the case of Damon—the wonderful gift of prolific and inventive inspiration ("Muse fertile" / "fertile veine"). The disgruntled Damon, however, is a washed-up relic characterized by the emphatic passé simple in v. 2 of *Satire I,* whereas the singular and divinely incorporeal Molière ("*Rare* et fameux *Esprit*") is unconstrained by the painful exertions that flesh-and-blood poets must suffer.[13]

Distinctions between the *passé* Damon and the celebrated Molière extend as well to their circumstances, provenances, and destinations. In contradistinction to the fictional (?) Damon,[14] who is fleeing from the moral and cultural abyss that he sees in Paris, Molière has pursued the reverse itinerary. After fourteen years of touring the provinces, his arrival on the Parisian literary and theatrical scene in 1658 makes him a kind of anti-Damon who has found fame and fortune in a city that Damon has been forced to leave, "chargé de sa seule misère" (*I,* v. 10). Whereas for Damon the capital and its denizens threaten to restrict his freedom within the four walls of a prison cell (*I,* v. 14), for Molière the road of life and art remains unimpeded: Apollo's wide-open treasure chest (v. 3) adumbrates the unrestricted freedom of "movement" ("Jamais au bout du vers on ne te voit broncher" [v. 8]) that Molière enjoys in his quest for *rime.*

In effect, Damon's fate, redolent of disharmony, discord, strife—of endless hindrances—can be reduced to his inability to find "rhyme" or, indeed, reason in the milieu in which he unhappily finds himself. His raging diatribe in *Satire I* communicates his reaction to this state of disequilibrium. Molière, who gracefully prevails in all "combats d'esprit" (v. 5) in which he must engage in his seemingly effortless pursuit of *rime,* becomes for the speaker an icon of perfection in art as well as in life. The speaker's deficiencies reinforce the gaping divide that separates the great Molière from all other poetic pretenders, here epitomized by the speaker, by the even more hapless Damon in *Satire I,* and later in this poem by a mob of lesser scribblers with neither talent nor taste.

Accordingly, in the guise of an aspiring initiate, the speaker humbly entreats the sainted Molière to teach him how to discover this core of harmony that is *la rime.*[15] Not unlike divine grace, rhyme appears to be sent from a mysterious external power (Apollo and "tous ses tresors ouverts" [v. 3]) that seeks out and touches the chosen few ("On diroit, quand tu veux, qu'elle te vient chercher" [v. 7]).[16] The penitential resonances of the speaker's yearning—who, "pour mes pechez" (v. 12), must practice this "rude métier" (v. 13)—echo *Satire I*'s manipulation of devotional terminology to depict Damon's flight from the "world." That the speaker has been coerced into becoming a "Rimeur" (v. 12) implies more than simply his ambition to exercise the poet's craft with less travail.[17] The quest for *rime* extends beyond the realm of the aesthetic to encompass social and moral considerations as well. Satirical poets like Damon (past), Molière (present), and the struggling, apparently neophyte speaker (future?) continually scrutinize and subsequently castigate their morally and intellectually dull environment in order to juxtapose to this world the higher realm of *rime* and the *raison* that might illuminate the obscurities and incoherences everywhere around them. Molière emerges as one who can smoothly and effortlessly create elegant verses embellished with purposeful rhymes, i.e., one whose comedic works delve into and illuminate the essence of society's foibles.

The speaker, on the other hand, sees himself as the slow-witted plodder who has been condemned to craft his verses in expiation of his real or imagined sins. Nevertheless, his manifest contempt for the "quinteuse" (v. 16) who invariably furnishes him with a rhyme contrary to the meaning that "raison" intended, appears at the best misplaced. The verses in which he reproves the muse of *rime* as a fiendish tormentor are in fact a superb illustration of the satirist's art:

> Souvent j'ai beau réver du matin jusqu'au soir:
> Quand je veux dire *blanc,* la quinteuse dit *noir.*
> Si je veux d'un Galant dépeindre la figure,
> Ma plume pour rimer trouve l'Abbé de Pure:
> Si je pense exprimer un Auteur sans defaut,
> La raison dit Virgile, et la rime Quinaut.
> Enfin quoi que je fasse, ou que je veüille faire,
> La bizarre toûjours vient m'offrir le contraire.
>
> (vv. 15–22)

If the essence of satirical art resides in its playful, humorous yet judgmental, even aggressive, attacks on generalized "dullness,"[18] these verses, with their "inappropriate" meanings produced by seemingly fractious rhymes, embody the indirect course that the successful satirist must pursue.

Indeed, the restive Pegasus portrayed by the speaker in vv. 15–22 is in actuality the wellspring of his art. While pure reason in fact does equate "un Auteur sans defaut" (v. 19) with the immortal Virgil, the antiphrastic bent of the speaker's poetic *modus operandi* imposes the antithetical Philippe Quinault, just as the wretched Abbé de Pure ludicrously turns up in his tortured mind as the very image of a young *galant.* The speaker's distress might be considered an elaborate pretense, since a more acquiescent rhyming muse would create works altogether distinct from his normally trenchant verses, full of irony and misdirection. In spite of the speaker's will to find "suitable" rhymes, *la rime*'s obstinate contrariness serves him well.

Although the speaker's anguish provokes within him the desire to abandon poetry and thus escape the accursed "Demon" (v. 25) that compels him to write, his muse unexpectedly yet unfailingly reappears: "Aussi-tost, malgré moi, tout mon feu se rallume: / Je reprens sur-le-champ le papier et la plume" (vv. 29–30). At these moments the erstwhile obstructed flow of rhymes becomes a furious torrent that he must strive to control. Not surprisingly, the rhyming muse's "verve indiscrete" (v. 33)—the epithet indicating a deficiency of judgment or discernment rather than the more modern sense of a want of tact or social restraint—creates for the speaker a new problem *opposite* in character from the preceding one. He now must exercise his *discrétion,* his own judgment and sense of correctness, in a word, his good taste, to compose his verses, since his inspiration, unlike his now prolific rhyming muse, will not tolerate "une froide epithete" (v. 34).

How simple composition would become if the discriminating speaker allowed his impetuous muse to supplant his better judgment! The speaker's "curse," however, is his oppressive need to adhere to an unspoken code of good taste. Just as vv. 15–22 exemplified the speaker's real dexterity as a versifier in spite of his explicit protestations as to the difficulty of his task and thus his incompatibility with his profession, vv. 37–42 ironically demonstrate his mastery of rhythm even as the skillfully accelerated cadence of the lines underscores the untoward speed with which the injudicious poet cranks out his meaningless rhymes:

> Si je loüois Philis, *En miracles feconde,*
> Je trouverois bientost, *A nulle autre seconde.*
> Si je voulois vanter un objet *Nompareil;*
> Je mettrois à l'instant, *Plus beau que le Soleil.*
> En parlant toûjours d'*Astres* et de *Merveilles,*
> De *Chef-d'œuvres des Cieux*, de *Beautez sans pareilles.*
> (vv. 37–42)

The result suggests an ironic tension between means and ends. The incoherent product foisted upon an undiscerning public by the Quinaults and Abbé de Pures of the world esteems quantity over quality: the dull poet transposes "*cent* fois et le nom et le verbe" (v. 45; my emphasis), whereas the poet of discretion (namely, the speaker) hungers for quality above all. In this laborious quest the poet must sift numerous rewrites in order to generate a valuable end result. The speaker's craving for compression and concision ("Si j'écris quatre mots, j'en effacerai trois" [v. 52]) engenders verses in which the "phrase insipide" (v. 49) has no place. Not for him the bland, "flavorless" amalgamations of the legion of facile poets who plagiarize Malherbe.

Unlike the Juvenalian first satire, *Satire II*'s Horatian inspiration is most evident at this point in the poem, for it recalls Horace, *Epistles* II.2, where the speaker extols the virtues of well-chosen, concise poetic language while lamenting his own proclivity to self-criticism:

at qui legitimum cupiet fecisse poema,
cum tabulis animum censoris sumet honesti;
audebit, quaecumque parum splendoris habebunt
et sine pondere erunt et honore indigna ferentur,
verba movere loco . . .

(vv. 109–13)

luxuriantia compescet, nimis aspera sano
levabit cultu, virtute carentia tollet,
ludentis speciem dabit et torquebitur, ut qui
nunc Satyrum, nunc agrestem Cyclopa movetur.
  Praetulerim scriptor delirus inersque videri,
dum mea delectent mala me vel denique fallant
quam sapere et ringi.

(vv. 122–28)[19]

Unfortunately for the lucid speaker in Boileau's poem, he knows all too well the rigors of poetic invention. The "Demon" that possesses him trammels his wish for peace and contentment. The happiness that he longs for, however, would come at the expense of his self-awareness. Without it he would be cast among that horde of writers who remain blissfully oblivious to the flaws in their shoddy writing. Boileau's contravention of Malherbian rhyme restrictions in vv. 61–62—rhyming two words belonging to the same family, *faire* and *affaire*—provides an ironic counterpoint to the speaker's bitter commentary on his lost peace of mind and sense of contentment in vv. 57–68.[20] This is precisely the sort of slipshod technique that the self-satisfied, careless poet—a "Pelletier" or a "Scuderi"—would foist on his readers. The fact that the speaker commits such an error in the middle of his regretful panegyric on the "good" life that he might lead were he a less exacting self-critic undercuts his sincerity. These two verses serve as examples of the craftsmanship of he who is "sans souci" (v. 61) and whose days might pass "pleins de loisir" (v. 58).

Instead, the bedeviled speaker will pass his days "cloüé sur un ouvrage" (v. 73, a veritable *calvaire!*) all because of his peculiar fixation on writing "poliment," that is, with polish, refinement, elegance. Presented as a virulent form of insanity ("cette frenesie / De ses noires vapeurs troubla ma fantaisie" [vv. 69–70]), the speaker's obsession detaches him from those "rational" authors—here represented by Pelletier and Scudéry—whose abundance is in inverse proportion to their worth. The speaker's apostrophe to "Bienheureux eri, dont la fertile plume" in v. 77 parallels the opening verse of the poem: in both lines the accent appears to be placed upon the repeated adjective "fertile," applying to both Molière and Georges de Scudéry, yet the key distinction of course devolves upon the nouns. Anyone (any hack) can purchase and wield an effusive "plume," but Molière's "veine" stands as a extraordinary gift from Apollo (v. 3) to a signal member of the poetic elite.

Indeed, "rational" poets like Scudéry appear to the imperceptive observer to be perfectly reasonable. Because their numerous works find eager sellers and buyers, public approval seems to refute the speaker's charges. His minority status tends to accentuate his "madness." Like the "Sots" who read them, the critical blindness of the Pelletiers and Scudérys—their lack of any sense of taste—has given them satisfaction and fulfillment. The speaker charges incoherence and lack of good sense, of *raison* ("Tes écrits, il est vrai, sans art et languissans, / Semblent estre formez en dépit du bon sens" [vv. 79–80]), yet everything in the Alice-in-Wonderland real world appears to confirm the contrary. Woe to the "demented" author who, like the speaker, has been cursed with good taste!

The speaker's problem thus goes well beyond his inward turmoil induced by his quest for the right rhyme as expressed in the beginning of the poem. In the external world of letters there exists a legion of literate "Sots," authors, book dealers, and readers alike, who have absolutely no inkling of what literary quality might encompass. The speaker's "madness" isolates him.[21] This curse is in reality, however, a blessing, for it permits him to recognize and to feel a kinship with a Molière, an "Esprit sublime" whose genius the speaker, at least, comprehends. Nevertheless, particularly galling to the speaker is a Scudéry's smug delight that he derives from the act of composition. The popular poet's obtuse self-adoration not only exacerbates the speaker's private torment, but also intimates the three-tier literary hierarchy suggested in the poem. At the summit dwells the truly exceptional Molière, described in vv. 91–94, who can boast of an immense coterie of admirers, who enjoys unequaled compositional facility, but whose own pleasure is spoiled by excessive autocriticism. On the intermediate level resides the speaker, another rare species, whose unerring sense of aesthetic "rightness" compensates for his compositional travails, heightened perception of his own artistic weaknesses, and apparent lack of any popular following. On the congested lower rung can be found the Pelletiers, Quinaults, Abbé de Pures, Scudérys, and others, whose supreme compositional ease produces numerous volumes appreciated by myriad readers, but whose critical vapidity will eventually relegate them to the ash heap of cultural history.[22] Despite this grouping and its ultimate implications concerning enhanced stature in the future, the speaker outwardly maintains his ambivalence toward his own immediately unhappy lot.

Satire II probes the societal status of the poet in relation to his personal happiness. The infuriating legions of tasteless "Sots," though stupidly happy with their lot while they are alive, will remain for all time the smug fools depicted here, thanks in part to the satirical poet. Their facile works cannot outlast the speaker's arduous efforts, since his infallible taste and judgment, although forcing him to undergo great anguish in his quest for the "correct" rhyme, will presumably allow his work to survive after his passing. In a more spiritual vein, true geniuses like Molière must sacrifice their earthly "repos" (v. 96) for a higher ideal. Analogous to the pious Elect, this tiny group will receive just recompense for its worldly isolation and sufferings.

In this vein, the speaker's final entreaty to Molière takes on the guise of a pious prayer directed to the patron saint of rhyme:

> Toi donc, qui vois les maux où ma Muse s'abîme,
> De grace, enseigne-moi l'art de trouver la rime:
> Ou, puisqu'enfin tes soins y seroient superflus,
> Moliere, enseigne-moi l'art de ne rimer plus.[23]
>
> (vv. 97–100)

Spiritually freighted words such as "maux," "s'abîme," and "De grace" in the last four verses reinforce this impression. Reminiscent of the preceding generation's poetic procedure, the poem's final *pointe* punctuates the speaker's playful solemnity throughout the poem. His paradoxical and misdirected request (how could the master rhymer teach another how *not* to rhyme?), if satisfied, would forever banish the speaker from the ranks of the Elect: it would ultimately lead not only to his artistic undoing but to his everlasting doom as well. After Damon's confidence-shaking diatribe and determined withdrawal from the poetic jousts of Paris, the brilliant example of a Molière must encourage the speaker to pursue doggedly his capricious muse. The speaker's feigned martyrdom in the name of taste and judgment in art will doubtless continue. Whereas Damon's determined quest for spiritual salvation implies his eventual artistic damnation, Molière's power as exemplum for the worshipful speaker, who must mortify the senses (cf. vv. 57–62) in his pursuit of enduring poetry, has in effect exorcised the influence of the diabolical "Damon" (pun no doubt intended) from the speaker's aesthetic psyche.[24]

A recurrent pattern of contrasting images reinforces Boileau's procedure of playful indirection in this poem. Such binary concepts as effort/ease, pain/delight, repose/struggle, search/discovery, order/disorder, quality/quantity, pieces/wholes, reason/folly, life/death, prison/freedom, sense/nonsense underpin the poem's metaphorical structure. The crucial dichotomy of good taste / bad taste, which more than any other lies at the foundation of this satire's thematic design, will be further examined in the ensuing poem.

Chapter Three

Nourishing Literature

"De gustibus . . . est disputandum"

From *Satires II* to *III* the focus shifts from the writer's domain—the conscientious speaker's tribulations in finding the right rhyme in his quest for poetic distinction—to that of his audience. *Satire III*'s burlesque account of a *repas ridicule* in fact explores the problem of aesthetic insensitivity in an audience whose already numb taste is further dulled by the plentiful literary slop served up by the likes of a Pelletier or the "Bienheureux Scuderi" so castigated in *Satire II.* The satirist can fulminate against this sad state of affairs, but improving the public's standards of taste remains an insoluble difficulty. The public's brutishness prompts the speaker's retreat from an arena in which his voice will not be heard, much less understood.

The art of cuisine might be thought of as the quintessence of metamorphosis, in that the *chef de cuisine* acts as a magician or a sorcerer, converting raw, unformed products of nature into an ordered, harmonious, and civilized array of courses and dishes that provide both pleasure and sustenance (*plaire et instruire*) to the diner. This creative process, wherein illusion triumphs over reality, is that followed by the artist, who establishes order from disorder for a clientele that will not only savor the result but also be changed by it. The notion of transformation thus extends to the consumer, who undergoes physical and moral change after consuming and assimilating the product. The progression from "unrefined" to "refined" centers particularly on the art of the writer, inasmuch as eating and poetry exist under the aegis of the mouth, into which physical nourishment disappears and out of which poetry emerges.

From the classical viewpoint, both literature and gastronomy operate under a system of more or less formal codification. The etymology of the word *gastronomy* (from *gaster,* "the stomach," and *nemein,* "to regulate") merely confirms this symbiosis.[1] In short, gastronomy and literature share a system of continua based on such concepts as taste, pleasure, consumption, transformation, creation, culture, and society. A celebrated contemporary cookbook, the anonymous L. S. R.'s *L'Art de bien traiter* (published in 1674; coincidentally, the same year as Boileau's *L'Art poétique*), defined in almost literary terms a kind of culinary classicism that stood in opposition to the unregulated and outmoded cuisine of the past.[2]

The banquet, that traditional social rite in which food, wine, and good conversation merge, provides the ultimate articulation of these elements.[3] Exploiting the metaphorical connection between gastronomy and poetry, Boileau actuates these oral activities in his *repas ridicule.* The disgusting food, insipid wine, and asinine conversation served up to the speaker in *Satire III* are exposed and scorned in his—oral—depiction and denunciation of the banquet made in response to his friend's opening question. Not surprisingly, the notion of orality thus stands as the predominate sign in this satire. The speaker treats his questioner to an intensely tasteless tableau in which all five senses come under relentless attack from a host of assailants.

In typical Boileau fashion, the poem is ostensibly a dialogue between A and P (*Ami* and *Poète?*). In actuality, P's long and picturesque response to A's opening questions and remarks makes up the body of the piece. Aside from the reaction to A's inquiry, little dialogical interaction occurs in the poem.[4] P's monologue describing the *repas ridicule* emphasizes his moral, if not physical, detachment from the host and his guests. P reports the conversation, such as it is, of the assembled *convives,* yet he consciously and perhaps understandably excludes himself from this interchange. The banquet, a social gathering ideally composed of *compagnons* (*com-* and *panis:* the word of course never materializes in the speaker's discourse), with whom one would joyously share bread as well as ideas, becomes rather a "Troupe serrée" (v. 53), words that evoke unwanted physical proximity as well as profusion. Despite the close quarters and the host's attempts to draw out the speaker (esp. vv. 116–28), he is speechless "comme une pierre" (v. 129) before this repulsive spectacle. He steadfastly maintains his nonparticipatory status as a perspicacious if not dispassionate observer with the power to retain and to recount what he has witnessed.

The concept of transformation, which underpins much of the metaphorical framework of the poem, is sufficient cause for A's opening query: "Quel sujet inconnu vous trouble et vous altère?" P's pale visage and somber mien contrast markedly with his usual rubicond, jovial self. The gastronomic ordeal that he is about to relate has indeed been a transforming experience, since his complexion formerly radiated the rare delicacies ("d'ortolans seuls, et de bisques nourie" [v. 6]) and shimmering fine wine ("le vin en rubis" [v. 8]) that he was wont to consume. Metamorphosis has also played a role in creating P's erstwhile healthy face: ingested by his body, the fruit of the vine, delicate birds, and a rich soup[5]—each dish presumably prepared with a blend of ingredients by a creative and skilled chef—have been first transformed from their natural state into gourmet delicacies, ultimately to effect profound and outwardly obvious change within the consumer. Now, his "air sombre et severe" exposes the revolting culinary and conversational fare served "chez un Fat" (v. 15).

The famous gastronome and chef Brillat-Savarin's dictum, "Dis-moi ce que tu manges, je te dirai ce que tu es," pertains particularly to the speaker in this poem.[6] If P's hearty appearance can be attributed to his sumptuous diet, it follows that badly prepared meals made with inferior ingredients, such as that served to the guests during the *repas ridicule,* will result in a defective constitution—both physically and intellectually. The succession of repugnant dishes described in this poem constitutes a syntax, carrying within it a system of signification. P's reluctance to partake of the feast reflects his fear that consuming third-rate food and drink will eventually transform him into a simulacrum of the host and his ravenous guests.[7]

Besides pointing to P's apparent rank as a man of taste and substance, A's reference to P's wines and melons having been ruined by overabundant rain conjures up a poetic backdrop associated with one of Boileau's so-called victims, Saint-Amant. This forerunner's many poems extolling the virtues of delectable wine and food ("La Pluye," "Le Fromage," "Les Goinfres," "Le Melon," etc.) were of course well known to the satirist. In one of these Epicurean works entitled "Le Melon," Saint-Amant's speaker celebrates the celestial qualities of a melon from which Apollo fashions his lyre.[8] Blending poesis and *gourmandise,* this self-reflexive poem containing an elaborate banquet scene connects the divine melon, wellspring of Apollo's art, to poetic inspiration and craft. P's link to melons can thus be taken to adumbrate his potential affinity with the art of Apollo.

More evident in *Satire III* is Boileau's debt to satirical predecessors who lampooned the comical food, drink, and loathsome company on similar social occasions, the best known of whom are doubtlessly Horace and Régnier.[9] As in his other satires in which a dialogical structure obtains, in *Satires* II.8 Horace presents a conversation between a character who bears his name, and presumably represents himself, and Fundanius, who in response to the character's questions describes a feast hosted by the wealthy Nasidienus. During this fools' feast replete with assorted parasites and lorded over by the pedantic and overbearing Nasidienus, a canopy collapses, ruining the host's highly vaunted fish dish. Fundanius eventually withdraws, vengefully refusing to taste the dishes presented to him. While Boileau's poem duplicates some of Horace's situations and themes, the Latin poet appears to focus attention on the foibles of the host Nasidienus, whose ludicrously inappropriate reaction to the canopy disaster and absurd belief that artfully prepared and presented food and superb wine might master destiny make him a prince of fools.[10] The unbiased critic could hardly accuse Boileau of plagiarizing Horace, as did so many of his inimical contemporaries.

Régnier's *Satire XI* provides another important source for Boileau's poem.[11] Eschewing the dialogue form, Régnier's piece is the monologue of a poet who has been coerced into attending the disgusting feast of a boorish host. In a wholesale assault on the reader's senses, the speaker's long and repulsive portrait of another guest, the *pédant,* leads to an equally repugnant description of the meal itself. A drunken brawl prompts the speaker's surreptitious retreat into a black, rainy night, from which he takes unforeseen refuge in a whorehouse. As with Horace's poem, Boileau's *repas ridicule* shares certain situations and themes with Régnier, such as the imperious host, the speaker's determined silence when faced with absurdly distasteful company and worse food and drink, the burlesque melee, and the speaker's abrupt and hasty departure. These surface similarities do not extend, however, to the pattern of images that underlies the poem's thematic structure.

A's expressions of curiosity and concern in vv. 1–13 introduce certain of these recurrent images, among them the notion of transformation: altered color and mood establish from the first lines a profound interplay between mind and body. The questioner conveys the belief that good cuisine is a matter of imposed rules and regulations, since only an official edict can "reform" the laws of gastronomy ("A-t-on par quelque Edit reformé la cuisine?" [v. 10]). The role of nature in the production of culinary raw materials receives its due in vv. 11–12, thus reinforcing the essential alliance between the natural world ("vos vallons") and the human domain as the foundation of culinary art. P's mouth-closing ordeal has lasting effects, since A's impatience at his friend's reticence ("Répondez donc enfin, ou bien je me retire" [v. 13]) must jar P out of his brooding silence.

The dramatic monologue in answer to A intimates from the first line that P's experience has been no less than life-threatening. His gasps for life-sustaining breath, rendered phonically by the repetitive [s] and the halting rhythms in vv. 14–16, accompany the overt mention of poison in the speech's second line. Persistent images of physical, intellectual, and emotional evasion and restriction associated with P's *res adversae* are evident in vv. 16–19 (". . . m'a forcé de disner," "J'éludois . . . sa poursuite obstinée," ". . . me serrant la main"). The host's promises of exquisite music ("Lambert . . . m'a donné sa parole" [v. 26]), wine to match, and the projected performance of the divine Molière ("*Rare* et fameux Esprit" [*Satire II,* v. 1; my emphasis]) convince the credulous speaker. The fact that Molière supposedly intends to play *Tartuffe,* the celebrated hypocrite, contributes to the aura of mendacity and deceit emanating from the blustering host. Despite the lurking danger for the less-than-usually wary P—who should have been alerted by the host's egregious name-dropping and this ironic allusion to a master creator of illusions, favorite playwright of Boileau himself—the speaker is lured by the "vaine promesse" (v. 29, "vaine" meaning *empty* in seventeenth-century French).[12] The speaker naively and unsuspectingly anticipates the promised entertainments. In v. 30 ("J'y cours, midi sonnant, au sortir de la Messe"), his eager dash from mass—ironically redolent of the spiritual, of salvation, of promises fulfilled—underscores the transformation that is about to take place: formerly a freely circulating, autonomous, and hopeful individual, the speaker will find himself in a place of restriction, personal vulnerability, and despair. His expectations of good company, good food and drink, good music, good poetry—a harmonious assortment of life's blessings—are dampened as soon as he enters his host's lair, where he is caught in the clutches of a man who will not give him up easily: "Mon Homme, en m'embrassant, m'est venu recevoir" (v. 32).

This image of constriction precedes the host's first broken promise. Not surprisingly, Lambert and Molière are nowhere to be found. As a consolation (booby?) prize, "Deux nobles Compagnards" replace the illustrious artists. The befuddled speaker accepts this metamorphosis with trepidation and much physical discomfort, for the room's infernal atmosphere parallels the intellectual ambience represented by the two country gentlemen. Like the meal to be served, this pair embodies the notion of quantity versus quality. These lovers of the interminable *précieux* novels so excoriated by Boileau pronounce "longs complimens" (v. 44) that induce rage—anger and irrationality—within the speaker. The speaker's reference to Mlle de Scudéry's *Le Grand Cyrus* underlines this artistic orientation. On greeting him, the host suggests a subtle correlation among Lambert, Molière, and the speaker ("Nous n'avons . . . ni Lambert ni Molière: / Mais puisque je vous voy, je me tiens trop content" [vv. 34–35]), and also implies that P's name has been used to entice the other guests ("Entrez. On vous attend" [v. 36]). The speaker's fury is hardly surprising!

The room set aside for the feast, a "Lieu de plaisance," becomes in P's depiction a kind of hell on earth, a *huis clos* with its closed shutters (v. 39) and second-story location (v. 38). Nature itself conspires against this accursed place: the personified "Soleil irrité" (v. 39) burns to punish the assembly. The sun's obvious mythological association with Apollo, god of music, poetry, and divination, again invokes the literary domain. His wrath, with an apparent desire for vengeance, serves to devalue further this social gathering and prefigures the "blasphemous" literary opinions that the guests will propound.

The poem's subsequent section introduces the actual meal. Transformation plays a prominent role in this motley cortege of dishes. The opener, a *potage,* in seventeenth-century usage a dish of meat and accompanying sauces, is metamorphosed, by almost unanimous popular acclamation, from a presumably tough and dry old rooster into a young and succulent capon:[13]

> Un coq y paroissoit en pompeux équipage,
> Qui changeant sur ce plat et d'estat et de nom,
> Par tous les Conviez s'est appellé chappon.
>
> (vv. 46–48)

The magic of language has effected this enchantment. Indeed, the numerous guests have likewise transmuted themselves, becoming nomenclators, possessing the ability to designate and thus to *re-create,* at least in their own minds, the inferior cuisine set before them. Alone in his refusal to accept this alteration, the speaker sets himself apart, reluctant to acquiesce in what for him is the falsification of reality, of nature.

Quite appropriately, immediately following the reinvented *potage* appears "une langue en ragoust de persil couronnée" (v. 50). Rabelaisian undertones accompany this sovereign ("couronnée") attraction. The tongue—symbolic of language, speech, of both literal and figurative taste, indeed of all the oral arts—finds itself transformed from a divine organ to a debased inanimate object, a sacrifice made to the assembled fools.[14] Served simultaneously ("Deux assiettes suivoient" [v. 49]) with an ill-prepared and mean pâté,[15] this most noble of organs has been shockingly desecrated. Celebrated under the sign of a lifeless, revolting tongue crowned not with laurel but with lowly parsley, the *repas ridicule* will play itself out, an unrelenting onslaught on the stunned eyes, ears, nose, tongue, and fingers of the trapped speaker.

Constrained first by the host's obstinate pursuit ("Depuis près d'une année" [v. 17]), by his grasp (v. 19), his embrace (v. 32), then his "chambre haute" (v. 38), the speaker finds himself squeezed by "nostre Troupe serrée" (v. 53) as the festivities truly begin. The word *troupe* connoting in this context an unruly throng, the guests crowd unceremoniously around a square table.[16] Again, quantity triumphs over quality at this gathering. For P such literal elbow-rubbing with this tasteless mob is an insufferable personal affront that degrades his sense of self-worth. Functioning on both literal and figurative levels, humiliating constriction and potential suffocation displace the speaker's former freedom of movement (v. 18, v. 30). Indeed, all is out of joint, "de costé" (v. 56), at this feast of fools.

Mocking allusion to Charles Cotin's and Jacques Cassagne's sermons provides associative transition to the poem's next section, where the host in turn delivers a kind of sermon, at least as preposterous as those of the sacred orators, exhorting the multitude to savor a soup made of lemon juice, egg yolks, and verjuice. Verjuice, the juice of unripe grapes, was still utilized by contemporary chefs, yet fashionable trends in the art of cuisine tended to move away from the medieval taste for highly acidic dishes.[17] Although in his notes Le Verrier asserts that this soup was a speciality of the cabaret Escu d'argent located at the place Maubert, its ingredients suggest strongly to this reader a culinary monstrosity. (Since Boileau implies in this poem that, the famous dictum notwithstanding, taste can in fact quite legitimately be disputed, this reader feels justified in making this summary judgment!) The host's overbearing insistence on approval increases the sense of constraint emphasized in the previous lines. The surroundings are physically and emotionally claustrophobic for the speaker.

Of course, a culinary creation requires a creator: Mignot, a contemporary "pâtissier et traiteur" (Ascoli 60), is raised to the status not of master chef but rather of master poisoner, a Medea-like figure (". . . dans le monde entier / Jamais empoisonneur ne sceut mieux son métier" [vv. 67–68]) who takes on a legendary eminence in the speaker's terrified imagination.

Ironically, given the orality of the occasion, P can answer his host only in gestures and mime; his customary verbal skills, evident in the very account of the feast, have been defeated. Like the hideous dead tongue sacrificed to the assembled revelers, the speaker's heretofore potent organ of speech has been neutralized. Such is the power of his adversaries, represented by the unspeakable host and his minions, a pair of ignorant and ill-bred "Campagnards," a "Troupe serrée" of parasites devoid of taste, and a gastronomic "artist" who poisons his clientele. This is a frontal attack on the tongue and all that it represents. The speaker's fear goes beyond his displeasure in bad company, food, and drink. Much more is at stake.

Despite all the signs to the contrary, ever hopeful that the wine will fulfill the host's promises, the speaker discovers that his full glass (quantity over quality) brought by a "Laquais effronté" (v. 72; all is "de costé") contains a mix of two inferior wines fraudulently sold as a high-quality *cru.* Besides being a second-rate *mésalliance,* an adulterated and thus "impure" concoction, the wine, like the company and the food, has been passed off for something that it is not. Its auspiciously vermilion hue conceals a tasteless, sickly sweet libation that deposits a harsh aftertaste on the tongue. His efforts to alleviate the wine's effect—adding water and searching for nonexistent ice in this inferno—result in rising indignation and the decision to withdraw in order to avert further depredations on his taste buds. Of course, the speaker's wish to flee from danger, however resolute ("Je me suis veu vingt fois prest à quitter la table" [v. 86]), cannot be realized in this *huis clos.* He is enmeshed in a fateful scenario, wherein a nightmarish parade of vile dishes, accompanied by poisonous wine, pass by in a predestined and immutable procession.

The sudden apparition of the *rost,* that is, the main meat dish,[18] commands the unflagging attention of each *convive.* Recurrent images distinguish P's description of this *défilé.* First, the sight of a misshapen heap of unfortunate creatures attracts the speaker's gaze (v. 93), accompanied by an attack on his nose (v. 92 and v. 99), then an incursion in his ears (vv. 101–02). As before, this onslaught violates his sense of autonomy; not unlike the "long cordon d'aloüetes pressées" (v. 94), the amassed guests form a similar *cordon* around the table. The plethora of animals sacrificed for this feast promotes the notion of quantity over quality. As in the first courses, popular acclamation transforms this inharmonious, incoherent stack of flesh, grease, and bone into a "superbe ordonnance" (v. 102), just as the troop itself undergoes an abrupt transfiguration: "Tous mes Sots à l'instant changeant de contenance / Ont loüé du festin la superbe ordonnance" (vv. 101–02).[19]

General, unparticularized enthusiasm for the various "morceaux" (v. 108) becomes personalized in vv. 105–14. Characterized by his oralism, a loquacious parasite, "à la gueule affamée" (v. 105), provides picturesque counterpoint to the mute, fasting speaker. Like the faceless mass gathered around the table, the "Hableur" (v. 105), a self-proclaimed gastronome, alters the nature of the dishes served: ordinary pigeons and rabbits become extraordinary delicacies through the magic of his active but insensitive tongue. Especially galling to the speaker, his obsequious flattery of the host again centers our attention on this prandial commentator who, choruslike, intervenes periodically to prod and thus further constrain the ever more isolated P.

Magically transformed by his guests' concord of praise ("nostre Hoste *charmé*" [v. 115; my emphasis]), the host betrays his dreadful taste when he boorishly applauds his own repast. The distinctive flavor of nutmeg appears to dominate all the dishes indiscriminately (v. 119). Moreover, the host's favored seasoning for sauce, pepper ("Quand on parle de sauce il faut qu'on y raffine, / Pour moi, j'aime surtout que le poivre y domine" [v. 126]), reeks of the parvenu, whose unrefined taste buds are capable of detecting only the coarsest of spices. Pepper's primacy among all other spices during the (primitive for Boileau) Middles Ages could not enhance the speaker's impression of his host's taste (Wheaton 15). Seventeenth-century trends in gastronomy were in fact renouncing former generations' fondness for heavily spiced food. Contemporary accounts from travelers express a marked distaste for the excessive doses of pepper, nutmeg, saffron, clove, and cinnamon in the food of other European countries.[20] Boileau would surely have subscribed to the tastes of L. S. R., who, in his 1674 *L'Art de bien traiter*, specifies the recent revolutionary changes in French cuisine:

> Ce n'est point aujourd'huy ce prodigieux regorgement de mets, l'abondance des ragouts et des galimafrées, la compilation extraordinaire des viandes qui composent la bonne chère, ce n'est pas cet entassement confus de diverses espèces, ces montagnes de rosts, ces changemens redoublés d'assiettes volantes et d'entremets bizarement servis . . . qui font l'objet le plus sensible de la délicatesse de nostre goust, c'est bien plutost les choix exquis des viandes, la finesse de leur assaisonnement, la politesse et la propreté de leur service, leur quantité proportionnée au nombre des gens, et enfin l'ordonnance générale des choses qui contribue essentiellement à la bonté et à l'ornement d'un repas, où la bouche et les yeux trouvent également leurs charmes . . . [21]

P's host is conspicuously ignorant of these fashionable trends. The host's large stock of pepper—second-rate seasonings wrapped in third-rate literature (vv. 127–28)—again focuses on Boileau's obsession with quantity prevailing over quality.

Contiguity of pepper and Pelletier bolsters the connection between cuisine and literature that forms the heart of the poem. Whether Boileau was thinking of the Italian troupe's staging of *Festin de Pierre* or rather of Molière's *Dom Juan*, the allusion to the Don Juan myth brings into play an evocative literary and social backdrop. The statue of the Commandeur eventually comes to life, wreaking vengeance on his wicked son, who is cast into hell at the end of the play. This reference bespeaks a burlesque analogy between Don Juan and the "sinful" host, the second of whom richly deserves the legendary seducer's fiery fate. This is only just, since he has inflicted hellish tortures on the speaker, who, like the numerous women seduced by Don Juan's lying tongue, has been lured and suborned by the host's false promises. The reader is present as the speaker "comes to life" in the beginning of the poem and launches into his tirade. His transformation from victim to potential avenger injects the theme of revenge, which, after all, is one of the goals of his long monologue and, indeed, of all satiric poetry. In effect, the oral punishment—bad food, conversation, wine, and so on—inflicted upon him is repaid in the speaker's oral reprisal. Simply stated, badmouthing begets badmouthing.

At this point, however, P's mute reply (". . . j'avalois au hazard / Quelque aîle de poulet, dont j'arrachois le lard" [vv. 131–32]), simply increases his sense of humiliation. The fleshless wing becomes a memorable, if nauseating, metaphor for the somatic and psychic insults he must swallow. The symbolic resonances of the wing take on some significance here. Otherwise associated with the poet's inspired elevation toward the sublime, a spiritual transcendence of the ignoble world here below (angels' wings, Pegasus's wings, Mercury's wings, etc.), the speaker's dead, denuded *chicken* wing, like the tongue served at the beginning of the meal, debases this exalted imagery and further condemns the feast. This is a place of profanation and sacrilege: under the aegis of the odious host, this noble symbol of poetic inspiration and *fureur* has been transformed into a thing of disgust and ridicule.

In marked contrast to the speaker's silence, the "Hableur" and his "voix haute" in v. 133 signal the next part of the poem, in which the assembled *troupe* begins to feel the effects of the barely potable wine described in vv. 73–78. With their grimy, overflowing glasses, the fools drunkenly compensate for the disappointing absence of the promised musician Lambert. Their "chanson bachique" (v. 142), harmoniously disharmonious ("Détonnant de concert" [v. 144]), again sets the unruly mob against the solitary speaker. These off-key lucubrations fittingly serve as music to accompany the not-so majestic *entrée* of the next course.

Once more the main dish undergoes transmutation, becoming a succulent and much-desired ham prepared in the manner of Mainz.[22] In ironically comparing the bizarre cortege to a learned university procession, the speaker emphasizes the oafish ignorance surrounding him as well as the ludicrously respectful demeanor of the valet (becoming the rector) and the "Deux marmitons crasseux" (becoming "Massiers") who attend. Not surprisingly, this wondrous spectacle provokes a change in the mellifluous revelers. Inexplicably, the mishmash of ham, mushrooms, sweetbreads, and peas produces a more serious, dignified mood. Fueled by alcohol, the guests transform into a circle of long-winded political, military, and, finally, literary authorities.

It is significant that the speaker devotes a mere eight verses to their meaningless exchange on current events, in which the drunken *convives* "resolve" the crucial political problems of the time, whereas his narration of their discussion of literature, which includes numerous direct quotes, contains forty-five verses. From this it seems safe to infer that P pays greater heed to the *troupe*'s opinions on contemporary authors and their works, confirming that the speaker is an author himself, or at least a dedicated devotee of the literary and theatrical arts. The guests, swollen not only with food and wine but also with self-assurance ("enflez d'une nouvelle audace" [v. 169]) after their victory over Holland and England, turn their expertise to an even more perplexing issue, that of formulating aesthetic judgments. In oral terms, the half-baked opinions that exit from the assembled mouths equal the ill-prepared, fraudulent, impure hodgepodge that has gone into them. The speaker's refusal to partake not only sets him apart from this undiscerning mass, but also suggests the danger of contamination, of corruption, that participation in such a fools' feast poses for the individual of taste. The famous adage "You are what you eat" might be extended here to "You *say* what you eat."

Not surprisingly, the assembled "Sots" lionize poets anathema to Boileau, i.e., Ronsard and Théophile de Viau, and mouth paeans to the equally detested Chapelain, René le Pays, Jean Puget de la Serre, and especially Philippe Quinault. Naturally, Pierre Corneille and Vincent Voiture, poets genuinely respected by Boileau, here receive only calumny. That this coterie of literary critics also scorns a certain "jeune homme" (v. 190) valorizes Boileau's own *Satire II,* placed on the same "negative" plane as the works of Voiture and Corneille. The guests' very awareness of Boileau's preceding poem further embellishes his reputation as a generally recognized literary commentator—even among a gathering of presumedly ignorant "Sots." The stress on Quinault's hollow sentimentality ("Et jusqu'à *je vous hais,* tout s'y dit tendrement" [v. 188]) and frivolous excess ("Et chaque acte en sa piece est une piece entiere" [v. 198]) accompany critical narrow-mindedness and shallowness (vv. 199–200). Ingestion of culinary rubbish leads to regurgitation of intellectual rubbish.

Descriptive correspondence between the food served and the literary convictions of its consumers further underscores the analogy between literature and cuisine. The host's apparent preference for one dominant taste in a particular dish, i.e., either pepper or nutmeg (vv. 119 and 126), coincides with the one-note penchant for *tendresse* (vv. 176, 178, 186–88) and the fixation on a single author ("Je ne puis souffrir ce que les autres font" [v. 199]). The superficiality of the works admired in this company ("Il est vrai que Quinaut est un Esprit profond" [v. 200]) replicates the ostentatious presentation of the inedible food and the extravagant reception given to it (vv. 46–48, 101–02, 149–54): a classic case of *paraître* over *être*. Finally, the ever-present compulsion for quantity over quality again emerges. The guests' preference for textual prolixity (vv. 43–44, 178–79, 198) parallels the lavish profusion of food served to the assembled *gourmands*. Clearly, aesthetic taste may be defined in terms analogous to those used to define culinary taste.[23]

In the poem's concluding section, the principle of orality—eating, drinking, talking—that has ruled the proceedings disintegrates, ironically, with the intervention of a representative from the realm of the *langue,* the fatuous poet in vv. 201–03. In a fit of drunken and jealous pique, he attempts to kill further discussion, suggesting an alternative, and perhaps preferable for everyone involved, oral activity: "Vous? Mon Dieu, mêlez-vous de boire, je vous prie" (v. 210). The *Campagnard's* quick and effective rebuttal dispenses entirely with words: ". . . et sans plus de langage, / Lui jette pour deffi, son assiette au visage" (vv. 213–14). The resulting mock-heroic melee substitutes outlandish action for equally outlandish words. Thus the banquet, ordinarily a locus of communality, friendship, and good cheer, has here degenerated into a vulgar brawl, a fitting end to a gathering of uncouth oafs. For its crude tastelessness, this physical interaction matches the preceding verbal and gustatory interaction.

As before, P maintains unyielding separation between himself and the ongoing events. Among the *convives* a manner of speech gradually returns; incoherent cries (v. 226) turn to words of reconciliation. Unfortunately, this does not bode well for the speaker, who must see this renewed harmony among the partisans of bad taste as dangerous to the forces of good taste that he represents. Implied in this *rapprochement* is the idea that good taste must forever struggle against a formidable and united front of those devoid of taste. Ever silent ("J'ai gagné doucement la porte sans rien dire" [v. 230]), P withdraws, swearing, in alimentary terms, never again to be trapped in such an alarming predicament. The series of oaths with which the poem closes merely illustrates his resolve, for denying oneself good wine, winter game (i.e., relatively rare), and out-of-season peas (quite the rage and very expensive in seventeenth-century France; see Wheaton 136) would mean the eventual annihilation of his personal good taste, both culinary and, understood in the context of this poem, aesthetic and social. Contact breeds contagion.

Despite the dangers of contamination, the speaker in this poem embodies the immutable and universal principle of right reason, with its corollary of good taste, which must continually struggle against transitory, individual judgments.[24] The speaker withdraws, yet his retreat is far from an admission of defeat. Although he was steadfastly silent at dinner, continued silence is unthinkable: it would mean yet another victory for bad taste.[25] The speaker's subsequent proclamation of derision and contempt, which we read as Boileau's *Satire III,* emerges as the supreme weapon against *mauvais goût*. His desensitized adversaries suffer from a kind of blindness that prevents them from seeing the light of reason.[26] Their enthusiastic acceptance of dishes that the speaker plainly sees as unworthy of human consumption, and their willing and self-deluding transformation of these dishes into not only palatable but delectable *friandises,* merely underscore their essential insensitivity. The defender of *raison* must warn others of this affliction. While the nameless horde arrayed against the isolated speaker at this dinner constitutes an omnipresent threat to *bon sens* and *bon goût,* the power of reason, wielded by such unwavering champions as P, ceaselessly resists this onslaught. The speaker's solitary unity must contend with the inferior plurality represented by the numberless other guests at this banquet.

A literary credo in the guise of an amusing and light-hearted burlesque, *Satire III* affirms the utter seriousness of Boileau's defense of his value system. By avoiding an impassive appeal to reason, his use of the culinary/literary metaphor asserts the power of emotion, of gut feeling, in poetry. The legion of "Fats" who see a marvelous feast in an ostentatious, immoderately lavish, and incoherent mess of ill-prepared food (read literature) is the greatest obstacle to the triumph of good taste. Their attack on the senses extends not merely to the speaker but to the reader as well. *Caveat lector.*

Chapter Four

Reason, Nobility, and the Pursuit of Happiness

We cannot conclude that the speaker's consistent silence during the wretched dining experience in *Satire III* is absolute, since the invective contained in the third *Satire* itself corroborates the systematic degradation of taste and reason in contemporary society. Boileau's savage frontal assault on the forces of dullness in *Satire III* softens, however, in the ensuing poem, *Satire IV.* Following a long tradition, especially in satirical poetry, this meditation on folly's universal dominion questions many of the assumptions that the speaker so vigorously and unquestionably espoused in the preceding poem. Reason, that stolid queen of human faculties, emerges as something less than an omnipotent guide in this poem.

Among Boileau's literary contemporaries, reason and taste were closely allied. To accuse one is to incriminate the other. If reason is not to be trusted as a standard for judgment, what then of individual taste?[1] Thus the speaker's uncompromising and perhaps self-righteous certitude that he is just and reasonable in his reaction to and evaluation of the company and cheer dished out at the *repas ridicule* changes in this poem to self-doubt and skepticism. The dialectical structure of the poem reflects the speaker's antithetical attitude toward reason's role and function.

As others have pointed out, the identity of the dedicatee lends to the work a strong sense of the *libertin* milieu.[2] The poem honors the Abbé le Vayer. Son of the well-known Pyrrhonian philosopher La Mothe le Vayer, he was a friend of both Boileau and Molière. Le Verrier claims that *Satire IV* was composed immediately after *Satire II*'s homage to Molière, and that it grew out of a conversation with Le Vayer *fils* and Molière on mankind's *folie.*[3] The poem's cynical view of reason's power reinforces this aura of *libertinage.* While the subject itself has been debated for many centuries—Horace, Juvenal, Montaigne, and Swift are among the many writers who have treated the subject—this skepticism in seventeenth-century France corresponds to *libertin* thinkers whose work Boileau most certainly knew.[4] Aside from reinforcing the dialectical associations prominent in the poem's developmental structure, the portrait of the contemporary freethinker in vv. 23–28—juxtaposed to the "Bigot orgueilleux" in vv. 19–22—enhances this impression.

In addition to possible *libertin* influence, Boileau's debt to Horace, *Satires* II.3, remains noteworthy. Horace's poem consists of a long speech addressed to a do-nothing poet outlining diverse vices that epitomize specific kinds of universal madness. Intended to impress on the addressee his own personal brand of insanity, this lively diatribe pays scant attention to the allied problem of individual gratification vis-à-vis irrationality so prominent in Boileau's conclusion. Another important forerunner is Régnier's *Satire XIV,* in which the speaker poses the elemental quandary confronting the judgmental satirist:

> C'est de nostre folie un plaisant stratagesme,
> Se flattant, de juger les autres par soy-mesme.
> (vv. 11–12)

Régnier emphasizes the popular dictum "chacun a sa raison" and asserts that *that* reason, although an "estrange beste" (v. 155), allows each individual in the human race to cleave to his or her particular conceptions of contentment. In this regard Boileau's poem owes more to Régnier than to Horace, since *Satire IV*'s thematic structure, notably in its conclusion, centers on private happiness. Paradoxically, the right thinking, "tasteful" mortal—not unlike the disapproving speaker at the *repas ridicule*—who maintains a clear-headed devotion to Reason and its ally, Taste, is in all probability incapable of felicity.

On another level *Satire IV* replicates the ancient tradition of the ironical encomium to folly, best known in Erasmus's 1511 *Stultitiae Laus.* In this complex work, Erasmus designates the rollicking banquet as locus *par excellence* for displays of folly among the gods if left undisturbed by the brooding Momus, god of reprehension.[5] Detached and alone, the Momus-like speaker in *Satire III* sits in judgment, listening to his reason.

After all, we learn in *Satire IV:* "C'est Elle [la Raison] qui farouche, au milieu des plaisirs" (v. 115).[6] Conversely, it is undeniable that the speaker cannot have pleasure where dullness reigns. What then is his source of pleasure, the wellspring of his own "douce manie" (v. 105)? Sneering at the saps around him, what else?! Boileau's insistence here and in other *Satires* that inner satisfaction, pure and simple, motivates his aggressive stance tends to downplay the importance of competing motivations. Leonard Feinberg has speculated on and summarized these possibilities as: aesthetic drive, vanity, pride, high moral purpose, revenge, rebellion, sadism, distorted self-criticism, and psychological and social adjustment. Boileau's enemies, of course, ascribed his gibes to a hostile, jealous, and essentially malicious character.[7]

Composed of a single question directed to the Abbé le Vayer, *Satire IV*'s opening section features the image of enclosure, or entrapment, that stands as a touchstone in much of the work. If the poem's main assertion is true—that we are *all* mad—then it follows that each of us exists in a *petite maison, incommunicado,* completely shut off from our neighbors. This self-perpetuating state of alienation stems simultaneously from within each individual—who, the speaker suggests, finds the rest of the world insane—as well as from without, from those "neighbors" who would sequester their fellows in the "Petites-Maisons" (v. 4), i.e., the asylums for the mentally ill. Recalling the speaker's detachment in *Satire III,* this inwardly/outwardly imposed isolation gloomily suggests that the individual's solitude will prevent communality of any sort—purpose, opinion, persuasion, taste, etc.—within the human race. What then is the fate of pervasive standards founded upon the concept of universal reason? More particularly, how can the speaker presume to judge the agents of dullness if he, unseeing, resides within the four windowless walls of his own psyche? Although merely suggested and introduced in *Satire IV,* this problem will be developed in subsequent satires.

The poem's initial four verses introduce a parade of familiar character types (vv. 5–28) illustrating the speaker's premise.[8] The Pedant, who is "enyvré," i.e., of impaired reason, displays psychological defects that reveal themselves in physical terms: his puffed-up outward appearance ("hérissé," "bouffi") encloses endless memorized (and doubtlessly misunderstood) quotations from "mille Auteurs," all "entassez" in his swollen head. His unequivocal reliance on Aristotle as reason's sole and infallible overseer confirms his innermost hollowness, despite his bloated facade.

The Pedant's narcissistic pretense matches that of the apparently dissimilar Galant, whose aimless and meaningless meanderings "de quartier en quartier" evoke the lightness of being made visible in his appropriately blond wig. Although the Pedant's mien suggested weighty profundity, his true emptiness aligns with that of the equally vacuous Galant. Paradoxically inducing fatigue and frigidity wherever he energetically alights, this ubiquitous denizen of the court flits about, dismissing real scholars while proudly wearing his own vacuity as a "titre d'esprit." Like Everyman portrayed in the poem's opening verses, who condemns his fellows to an imprisoning enclosure, the almost illiterate "perruque blonde" banishes the truly learned to another kind of enclosure, to "le fond" of an (educational) institution.[9]

Pretense, vanity, self-righteousness, and intrinsic emptiness extend as well to the next specimen in this cavalcade of fools, the *faux dévot.* The Bigot's "vanité" (cf. the Latin *vanus:* "empty" or "vacant"), masked by feigned holiness, presumes to deceive God Himself; he thus righteously appropriates God's own power to damn the rest of a faceless humanity. His "*pleine* puissance" (v. 22; my emphasis) ironically reinforces the true void deep within.

Just as the apparently antithetical yet essentially identical Galant succeeded the Pedant in vv. 11–18, a Libertin, conventional antipode to the Bigot, materializes in vv. 23–28. Appropriately, this character exhibits deep-seated similarities to his predecessors despite superficial differences. Possessing no genuine substance ("sans ame et sans foi" [v. 23]), the disdainful and arrogant freethinker clings to his own "suprême loi" (v. 24), of pleasure in his case, while dismissing the *dévot* as a weak, fainthearted creature who should be restricted within the "Petites-Maisons" reserved for true believers in the freethinker's own narrow mind. His wholesale condemnation of "tout Devot" (v. 28) mirrors the Pedant's, Galant's, and Bigot's contempt for the Other. For the Libertin, hell is a mere fairy tale, capable only of spreading terror among children and silly women. Whereas the *faux dévot* assumes unto himself powers appertaining solely to God, the Libertin takes the opposite tack, going so far as to deny his own spirituality ("sans ame"), thus disavowing his humanity and placing himself, ironically, among the unreasoning beasts. His conviction that all Christian believers have "le cerveau perclus" (v. 28) extends the enclosure metaphor, since the adjective *perclus,* signifying immobilization, deepens the speaker's impression that all of us are imprisoned within our own folly.

The comical procession of essentially identical fools, although presented in a dialectical pattern in vv. 5–28, might have continued *ad infinitum,* given the inexhaustible array of human types available to the satirist. Rather than endlessly listing "de tant d'esprits les diverses manieres,"[10] in vv. 29–34 the speaker shifts his attention to the nonspecific yet rampant folly within a faceless, nameless humanity. People's blind credulity comes to the fore here: profiteering charlatans in medicine and virtue enjoy equal acceptance among a gullible mass eager to purchase their respective wares. Whether the example be an individual type or a collective entity, the subversion of reason manifests itself indiscriminately. The insane individual, be it the Pedant, the Galant, the Charlatan, or any of the myriad other types, finds a perfect complement within the mob outside himself. Considered individually or collectively, humanity is mad.

Haunted by the familiar quality/quantity dichotomy, the speaker is aware of the interminable and inevitably rambling catalog of illustrations of his major premise that he could generate; thus in vv. 35–36 he self-consciously comments on his own procedure and the paradoxical trap the judgmental satirist might fall into. His repetitive ramble into "vagues propos" (*vague* carrying the sense of empty as well as indistinct) might cast suspicion upon his own faculties of reason, for how can the satirist escape the general condemnation that he himself has enunciated in his poem? His succinct "deux mots" in v. 36 actually means two verses, 37–38, in which he encapsulates the general proposition that true wisdom, even among the hallowed "Sages de Grece," cannot exist in this contingent world of decidedly imperfect human beings. The speaker emphasizes his own precarious position as self-proclaimed *sage:* If indeed we are all travelers hopelessly lost within the unfathomable forest of our own flawed psyches, who has the right to call anyone else a fool?

On the other hand, the speaker adroitly legitimizes the seemingly contrary notion that a guide might exist who could attend to the disoriented traveler: "Les voyageurs *sans guide* assez souvent s'égarent" [v. 42; my emphasis]).[11] Thus he admits the possibility of useful guidance, but this beacon of reason must first direct his ray of critical discernment within. To master the art of self-reproach in a humble and sincere attempt to arrive at self-knowledge remains as prerequisite to the satirist's enterprise. The closing verse of this section, however, soberly acknowledges the challenge for the speaker, since ". . . chacun pour soi-mesme est toûjours indulgent" (v. 59). Naturally, rare is the person who—like the speaker in *Satire II* and unlike Damon in *Satire I* and P in *Satire III*—dwells on his/her own defects.[12]

The primary dichotomy of the inner and outer worlds, expressed in terms of purported lucidity in regard to the external and utter blindness to the dynamics of one's own psyche, receives additional elucidation in vv. 60–71. The speaker devotes six lines each to those hoary conventional figures, the Miser and the Spendthrift. The contradictions inherent in each type find ample and succinct corroboration in the vocabulary: "disette"/"abondance," "folie"/"prudence," "bien"/"rien," "Plus"/"moins," "importune"/"fortune." That the wealthy profligate comments disparagingly on the rich skinflint merely accentuates the universal folly/blindness basic to the poem's thematic structure. The reflexive nature of the contemptuous interplay among individuals exempts the speaker, who castigates mankind, yet avoids pointing to the disdain that the Other must assuredly have for him. Does he exercise the judicious restraint toward others so warmly endorsed in vv. 54–58? Is he blind to his own flaws? His own example seems to confirm the poem's opening premise.

The inveterate Gambler—otherwise "sage et prude"—portrayed in vv. 72–84 instantly and correctly perceives the insanity of the Miser and the Spendthrift. Despite their apparent differences, these three *fous* adhere to the pattern exemplified in vv. 5–28 and postulated in v. 44: each has fabricated a source of supreme personal felicity that supplants all others. Not unlike the diners in *Satire III,* each has the capacity of transforming outer reality in accordance with personal desire or opinion.

As in *Satires I* and *II,* spiritual terminology plays a key role in these sketches. The Miser is an "idolâtre" whose worthless riches comprise his "souverain bien"; the Spendthrift's "âme inquiete" agonizes over its equally worthless wealth; the Gambler's luck, according him "vie" or "mort," causes him, if bad, to imprecate heaven itself, "Ainsi qu'un possédé que le Prestre exorcise." The speaker sees these fools, each motivated by the root of all evil, as insanely confused between heaven itself, mankind's ultimate spiritual aspiration, and the blinding object of his obsession, i.e., amassing, bestowing, or winning money. As in *Satire I* depicting Damon's penitential retreat from the worldly evils of Paris, the satirical target takes on convoluted spiritual overtones.

In vv. 85–89 the speaker's roster of blind fools changes direction, moving away from the realm of lucre to confront the literary. Whereas the Miser, Spendthrift, and Gambler suffer grievously—and justly—from their respective follies, there remains a species of fool who actually savors the "aimable poison" whose inebriating "charme" relieves him of good sense.[13] Like the dead who drank from the Lethe to forget the pain endured in life (v. 89), bad writers imbibe a "nectar" that confers the joy of blessed oblivion.

"Chapelain" incarnates this foolish, obtuse, yet happy poet. Like the happily voracious diners in *Satire III* or the "Bienheureux Scuderi" (v. 77) in *Satire II,* who tend toward the bloated, the insipid, and the incoherent (vv. 91, 97, 99), Chapelain (along with the others) resides in a land of Cocaine, unaware that "quelque Audacieux" (v. 95, i.e., the speaker—in the seventeenth century the word emphasized boldness rather than impulsiveness) discerns the dullness beneath the murk of his delusions. Herein lies the "audacious" character of the satirist, who may dare to "désiller les yeux" (v. 96) of the blind fools, thereby dissipating the blissful fog in which they move. Fortunately for Chapelain, his "ame insensée" (the epithet carrying the dual meaning of *irrational* and *misdirected*) can continue to wander (N.B. the double sense of "erreur" [v. 102]). No exception to the general rule, the deluded and talentless writer—like the rest of humanity, "voyageurs sans guide" (v. 42)—is lost in the trackless forest alluded to earlier (vv. 41–44).

Verses 103–12 provide an example of a fellow traveler who acquires a "guide" for whom he felt no need or desire. In this case another oxymoron—"douce manie" (cf. "l'aimable poison" of v. 87)—describes the magnificent obsession of another familiar type, the "Bigot, d'ailleurs homme sensé," who has attained oneness with a supposedly imaginary world of transcendent harmony. Healed of this "mal assez bizarre" (v. 104), the somewhat less than thankful true believer curses the doctor as an infernal agent dispatched by the devil to deprive him of heaven on earth, thus in effect damning him. Although the Bigot himself states that his feverish imagination created an "erreur" (v. 112), who can really say that his beatitude was merely a hallucination? Where does reason end and imagination begin? In this case individual happiness was sacrificed in the name of reason.[14]

As the perfidious instrument of reason, the doctor is no exception to the general rule of folly's sway over men. What right had he to destroy his patient's harmless illusions? Motivated perhaps by greed (vv. 109–10), his success in delivering his "deranged" patient from rapturous visions illustrates his own delusions of power and self-righteousness, the source of his happiness. He is analogous to the literary satirist, "quelque Audacieux," who would dare to open the starry eyes of the bedazzled Chapelain. Man's goal, after all, is to achieve contentment. Abstract standards of correct thought and behavior merely remind him that he is an imperfect, incomprehensible creature seeking a pitiable escape from despair.

The poem's ironic concluding section meditates on Reason's precise function. Reason's sermonizing minions, those who endeavor to "elevate" the human spirit, are doomed to failure. Human nature, inclined to gratify base hungers, will not listen to this "Fâcheuse," this "Pêdant," who never tires of heaping opprobrium on man and his follies.[15] The eternal reign of what may be termed dullness has a simple, yet powerfully effective *raison d'être:* man's unrelenting pursuit of happiness, which has no basis in reason. The doctor in the case of the Bigot, the preacher Joli (v. 120), and indeed the speaker/satirist in the first part of this poem will forever encounter indifference and disdain from those whom they wish to purify. These petty tyrants will never "cure" man.

Thus the speaker's purpose has evolved from a smug denunciation of man's neglect of reason to a condemnation of Queen Reason herself. The faults ascribed to the tedious Pedant who opened the list of conventional exempla affirming the speaker's premise are reprised in the close of the poem. The Pedant's bookish ignorance, air of superiority, and absolute self-possession (vv. 5–10) duplicate Reason's very own manner and preachments. Propagated by "Rêveurs"—i.e., ironically those unconfined by the boundaries of rationality—Reason emerges as an illegitimate pretender to sovereignty (v. 121) and even to divinity (v. 123), a false prophet who preaches wisdom and contentment gleaned from books (v. 126) but who has no appreciation of the reality of the human condition. The man of discernment (our speaker), while respectful (v. 127), can nonetheless see through Reason's seductive ("fort beaux" [v. 126]) allure.

The speaker's observations and interpretations of the world about him thus extend to the instrument by which he performs this analysis. He is no exception to the general rule enunciated in vv. 38–40:

> En ce monde il n'est point de parfaite sagesse.
> Tous les hommes sont fous, et malgré tous leurs soins,
> Ne different entre Eux que du plus ou du moins.

The speaker's personal "douce manie" turns out to be an all-consuming desire to detect deficiencies in whatever he examines. The result, anathema to the satirist, is a fluctuating position, expressed in tones ranging from contempt to envy, that belittles "l'homme le moins sage" in v. 1 only to conclude in the last verse that presumably the same individual—"le plus fou"—is in reality the most fortunate of men.

If developed and pursued, this skeptical *mise en cause* of his principal weapon Reason would put the polemicist/speaker in an untenable epistemological position. The poem's terminal verse accentuates, however, the notion of degree, evident in other sections of the poem. The portraits of vv. 5–34 offer examples of "l'Homme le moins sage" introduced in the poem's opening line. Verses 35–59 take another tack, emphasizing that all men may be fools, as the speaker unequivocally states in v. 39, but that some men are more foolish than others. Since there exists no "parfaite sagesse" (v. 38) among us poor mortals, there is on the other hand "Le plus sage" (v. 54), the individual supremely aware of his own failings, therefore less likely to denounce his fellows rashly (although this is undeniably impossible, given that "Tous les hommes sont fous"!). A second list of stock figures in vv. 60–84, illustrating the premise of v. 59 ("Mais chacun pour soi-mesme est toûjours indulgent"), precedes two crucial portraits, the dreadful writer and the illuminated believer, offering further cases of extreme folly. From this vision of hierarchical madness the speaker emerges as one who "veut se connaître" (v. 53). His concluding sympathy for the disgruntled Bigot—implicitly easing his rancor toward the assorted crazies described in the poem—reveals his penchant for "douceur" (v. 55) when judging his fellow beings. Without stating outright his compassion for the weak and deluded creature that is man, the speaker subtly conveys his understanding of himself as well as the Other. He may indeed not be "le plus satisfait," but more importantly, neither is he "le plus fou." Pleasure obviously can be had, but good taste must accompany indulgence of the senses or the mind. Genuine pleasure is intensified by good taste and by reason itself. Still, the speaker, in moments of weakness, may envy those who are unfettered by Reason's chains.

Though dealing with the struggle between individual contentment and *bon sens,* as does *Satire II,* this poem takes a different approach to the problem. In the former poem the writer/speaker's confident belief in the inevitable triumph of Reason, so that his present anguish may be justified in the name of future esteem, becomes less self-assured. The viewpoint expressed in *Satire II* and so clearly practiced in *Satire III*—the unspoken yet palpable conviction of his own moral, aesthetic, and social supremacy—is shaken in *Satire IV.* He does not see Reason, along with its ally, Taste, as an all-benevolent and immutable beacon of truth. This does not imply, however, that Queen Reason must be abandoned. Like all things human, she too has defects: the perceptive critic—"Le plus sage"—does not shrink from pointing out that even she has not attained "parfaite sagesse." Human reason, imperfect and relative though it is, might still aspire to deeper insight into the human heart.

This analysis of reason, folly, and individual contentment underscores the satirist's predicament. In moments of weakness a dangerous skepticism of all formerly accepted norms may creep into his ongoing social commentary, sowing doubt in a mind that must preserve certain fixed standards of judgment. Such self-scrutiny tends to exclude him from the ranks of all those, mentally lodged in "Petites-Maisons," who blindly appropriate wisdom unto themselves. The speaker's backing away from his absolute self-righteousness confirms the notion expressed in v. 54: "Le plus sage est celui qui ne pense point l'estre."

As a satirist but also as yet another inmate in the asylum, it can be said the speaker is *fou* in the same manner as the well-known fool figure of the Middle Ages and Renaissance, he who dared to criticize institutions, values, and beliefs that were normally off limits.[16] The word *fou* can, after all, take on a double meaning. Besides pertaining to man as madman, it may also refer to the literary character of the fool, especially the "artificial" fool of the Middle Ages and Renaissance, the *stultus,* the *ineptus* out of whose mouth wisdom comes.[17] On the other hand, all manner of "fools" rule society. While the so-called wise men attempt to perfect themselves and others, they tend to withdraw from this society, becoming caustic observers rather than actors. If all men are fools, to what purpose are criticisms that strive for the impossible—bettering man's condition? In this light, the sage is also a fool.

Satire V, which follows, rejects the relativism of *Satire IV* and insists on the legitimacy of abstract standards. The notion of a long, noble heritage that latter-day family members are obliged to emulate extends as well to the "family" of poets, among whom there exists a kind of aristocracy, a tradition of quality that honorable descendants like Molière uphold and that others, like the speaker, strive to equal. In the realm of satire, Boileau's patrician antecedents—Lucilius, Horace, Persius, Juvenal, Régnier—have established the example that he has the solemn duty to follow. He must continue on "la trace où marchoient ses ayeux" (*V,* v. 4), despite the myriad obstacles treated at length in *Satires III* and *IV.*

The universal themes that lie at the heart of *Satire IV*—that all men are fools, blinded by a "manie" (v. 105) that may engender discontent but more often produces contentment, that some men are less foolish than others, and that man judges his fellows in accordance with his own mental and emotional defects—were illustrated with numerous exempla affirming the speaker's thesis. The ensuing *Satire V* dwells at length on another example of man's folly not mentioned in the preceding poem, the mania of nobility. *Satire V* might partially be considered a continuation of *Satire IV*, for it offers a precise, detailed example confirming the general opinions expressed in *Satire IV.*

As in other satires, the concept of example pervades this poem not only as a partial description of its structural function within the corpus of Boileau's *Satires,* but also from the point of view of theme. The seventeenth century viewed nobility itself as the highest standard from which to evaluate social comportment.[18] As such, it falls into the same category as reason and taste. The speaker in this poem declares that the criterion of nobility derives from a long and distinguished chronicle of virtuous and honorable deeds that stand as documented evidence of exemplary human behavior. These patterns are legitimate, not originating in man's fevered brain ("Tous les hommes sont fous" [*IV,* v. 39]), but rather having their source in nature. Man's attempts to contravene these standards amount to a heinous crime against Nature. Degradation of this ancient norm of behavior results in a society in which man's endemic *folie* displaces higher concerns.

The notion of example goes hand in hand with the principles of quality and rank. In *Satire IV* the speaker claims that man's folly, though pervasive, allows nonetheless for marked degrees of insanity. The speaker thus postulates a fundamental hierarchy in which "le plus sage," although not the happiest of men, is possessed of a relative self-knowledge that places him on a higher level than the mass of blind fools around him. Aristocracy corroborates the fact that judgments concerning degrees of quality or lack thereof are not only possible but necessary in a society in which standards have become less susceptible of clear definition.

The theme of false nobility, of the distinctions to be made between intrinsic and extrinsic nobleness, has a long history in satirical poetry. According to Boileau's commentator Le Verrier, *Satire V* was composed just after the poet completed *Satire II* in honor of Molière, and before he began work on *le repas ridicule.* The major source for the poem appears to be Juvenal's *Satire VIII,* from which Boileau freely borrowed images and ideas, including the crucial racehorse analogy (vv. 56–67 in Juvenal). We hardly need mention Molière's contemporaneous *Dom Juan*[19] and the 1670 *Le Bourgeois Gentilhomme,* as well as La Bruyère's caustic wit in *Les Caractères,* to demonstrate the theme's appeal among Boileau's readers.

Structurally this poem contrasts with its predecessor. Unlike the unique addressee of *Satire IV,* this piece keys on two "noble" persons: one representing genuine nobility, the Marquis de Dangeau referred to in the first line; and his opposite number, the "grand Heros" (v. 25), that perfidious subverter of the ideals embodied in the paragon Dangeau. The pattern of address is straightforward: the speaker initially directs his speech to the noble Dangeau, then, in the body of the poem, in a long oration full of angry indignation, sarcasm, and outright insults, confronts the false noble. In the concluding lines he returns to Dangeau, adding, prudently, that that exemplar of true aristocracy, the King, must be the object of his subjects' unfeigned admiration and, therefore, emulation.

The King as prototype for "noble" comportment among his subjects is a further evocation of the analogy between the religious and the secular codes that we have seen propounded in the *Satires.* Just as the ultimate aspiration of the Christian life is the imitation of Christ, the speaker here suggests that the epitome of the noble life is the imitation of the King. The third verse, with its "Demi-Dieux," and v. 17, in its reference to "source divine," reveal the conventional poetic merging of nobility and divinity.[20] *Satire I*'s ironical identification of Damon with the penitent Christian withdrawing from the world, and the speaker's *calvaire* in *Satire II,* are earlier examples of Boileau's propensity to combine the sacred and the secular. The values promulgated in the *Satires* thus bear comparison to those of God Himself as revealed by the Church.

The speaker's apparently wavering stance on the merit and purpose of reason in its role as unimpeachable standard of wisdom in *Satire IV* is short-lived, for the very first verse of the following poem repudiates such permissive cynicism. As a standard for man's behavior, nobility does exist, despite its elusive impalpability. A fundamental element of *Satire V,* the relative values of the abstract and the concrete, opens the speaker's meditation. The speaker firmly declares the preeminence of the intangible throughout the poem. False nobles attempt to use the concrete to prove the abstract. The sage (our speaker!) knows how to differentiate the true from the false. In an effort to concretize the abstract, he depicts real nobility as an unbroken path leading from the past to the present. Men require a concrete example, namely, Dangeau, to envision the "étroite loi" and the "vertu severe" that have no material existence in this world.

The play of spiritual essence and visible facade is sustained in vv. 5–24, in which the ignoble "Fat" is defined in opposition to Dangeau. The speaker objectifies and thus debases the false noble: he is a shapeless, mushy mass in need of propping up ("mollesse" [v. 5], "lâche et molle" [v. 20]).[21] This necessity for exterior bolstering is acute, since his "noblesse," is "vaine," i.e., hollow. To conceal his empty core, he wraps himself in reputations and honor traitorously ("insolemment") stolen from others. He owes his substance to a most insubstantial material ("vieux parchemins" [v. 16]) and even to his allies, the worms, which did him the favor of sparing these pitiful remnants of his current prestige! His "gloire" is reckoned as a "vain amas," which echoes the imagery of vv. 5–6 in which the "Fat" was introduced. Past bears on the present only when there is a direct link between the two, as in the case of Dangeau, who follows "la trace où marchoient ses ayeux" (v. 4). The fraudulent nobleman, who has effectively cut himself off from the glory that emanated from his ancestors, can only display flimsy paper evidence ("vieilles chroniques" [v. 10], "vieux parchemins" [v. 16]) and meaningless emblems ("leur écusson" [v. 12]) as proof of his present worth.

Accompanying images of shapelessness, hollowness, softness, and flimsiness are recurring ironic allusions to divine origins. Verticality underlines the disparity between his "high" birth (v. 22), his "superbe origine" (v. 18, *superbe* indicating physical as well as moral elevation), "le Ciel" that appears to bow to his will (v. 23), and the lowly reality ("N'a rien pour s'appuier . . ." [v. 6], his association with the "vers" [v. 16]) of the character himself. Ironically, this "Fat" is indeed made from clay different from that of the speaker (v. 24): a vile, formless, indeterminate substance that is something less than animate ("S'endort dans une lâche et molle oisiveté" [v. 20]). This weak, flaccid, amorphous—almost wormlike—specimen of "high" birth is violently dehumanized by the inimical speaker.

The speaker's rising anger becomes immediately apparent in the ensuing long speech directed to the false noble himself. The peremptory imperative that begins the address sets the tone, reversing the accustomed social roles of noble and *roturier.* That the humble speaker commands the scion of "tant de Heros celebres dans l'Histoire" (v. 14) reinforces his sarcastic form of address to this modern "grand Heros, Esprit rare et sublime" (v. 25). The dehumanization of the "Fat" continues with the racehorse analogy contained in the speaker's confrontational question, especially in view of the "grand Heros" / "Animaux" rhyme at the caesuras of vv. 25–26. The heroic racehorse exhibits traits in diametrical opposition to those of the false noble just described in vv. 5–24. He is "*plein* de cœur" (v. 27), full of unflagging zest and power (vv. 28–29), and makes fully visible to all ("Fait paroistre en courant" [v. 28]) his excellence. In addition, the champion horse's exploits recall the poem's opening image (vv. 3–4) of energetic movement along a designated pathway: he is a "Coursier" (v. 27) who will never falter in his "carriere" (meaning *race,* or *trajectory* in the seventeenth century). Crowned with "noble poussiere" (v. 30), like the heroes of countless prior literary works—and quite unlike the "Fat" (one might imagine his dust-covered chronicles of erstwhile glory)—this paragon of noble equestrian achievement has established, through deeds, his natural, God-given nobility.

The speaker's emphasis on the animal world suggests the key role of nature in his meditation on nobility. His proposed definition of true quality focuses initially on its origins. The source of distinction lies within nature itself.[22] Nature provides the impetus, whether it be physical stamina, strength, or unbending will, qualities that in turn manifest themselves in traits that man esteems as moral such as courage, purity, and tenacity in the face of formidable opponents. Contrary to the contemporaneous doctrine of hereditary preeminence, these natural endowments do not necessarily pass from one generation to the next. For this reason man intervenes when racehorse progeny do not follow the "marche," or the "carriere," of their forefathers.

Cognizant of the noble line being broken or interrupted by unworthy offspring in the animal domain, man relegates such nags to a function more in keeping with their natural attributes (vv. 32–33). The tasks such animals may perform, ". . . porter la malle, ou tirer la charuë" (v. 34), correspond exactly to those performed by the so-called lower social classes. From this analogy the speaker's intention is clear: the "Fat" to whom this speech is addressed, should, by the rights of nature, trade places with his porter or indeed with the peasant plowing the fields on the nobleman's estates.

Although people are not deceived by an unworthy horse descended from a long line of champions, they remain blind to the identical happenstance among their fellow beings. The speaker, however, takes care to exempt himself from this common lack of insight: "On ne m'éblouit point d'une apparence vaine" (v. 37). As one undeceived by surface subterfuge, the speaker proffers in vv. 38–45 a concise blueprint for nobility. As with the racehorse analogy, here Boileau borrows from Juvenal's *Satire VIII,* vv. 56–67. Inspired by the Roman's dictum "Nobilitas sola est atque unica virtus" (*VIII,* v. 20), v. 38 in Boileau's poem ("La vertu, d'un cœur noble est la marque certaine") insists on the harmonious relationship between *être* and *paraître* in the aristocracy. The genuine article wears a "marque certaine"; he is called upon to reveal to the beholder's eye ("Montrez-nous cette ardeur qu'on vit briller en eux" [v. 40]) a shaft of blazing light ("ardeur" from the Latin *ardor,* "heat, flame"). This heat imagery repeats that just applied to the racehorse in v. 28: "Fait paroistre en courant sa *boüillante* vigueur" (my emphasis). The notion of law and its companion, justice, first alluded to in the poem's second verse, again comes to the fore in the questions the speaker pointedly asks in v. 42. The concept of resolute movement, so prominent in describing Dangeau and the champion racehorse in contradistinction to the torpid, immobilized "Fat," is reiterated here: "Fuiez-vous l'injustice?" (v. 42) and "Sçavez-vous pour la gloire oublier le repos?" (v. 43). Whereas the sham nobleman nods off "dans une lâche et molle oisiveté" (v. 20), the real aristocrat nobly sleeps "en plein champ le harnois sur le dos" (v. 44), unmistakably exhibiting to all his martial fervor, physical stamina, and bravery in the service of virtue. In the last verse of his definition the speaker repeats the key word, "illustres *marques*"—

external manifestations of inner qualities—which appeared in the opening line, v. 38. These "marks" of nobility are plainly visible to the discerning eye.

In his definition the speaker fixes our attention on the present at the expense of even the most illustrious pedigree ("Alors soyez issu des plus fameux Monarques; / Venez de mille ayeux . . ." [vv. 46–47]). This apparent repudiation of the concept of inherited quality can also be seen in Juvenal, who declares that it matters not who one's ancestors are when individual merit reveals itself (Boileau, vv. 48–52; Juvenal, *Satire VIII,* vv. 127–41). Conversely, noble birth becomes a powerful indictment against the unworthy "Fat," whose behavior makes plain to all the incongruities of past, ephemeral honor and present, manifest dishonor. The speaker imagines a body of ghostly witnesses, all testifying to the shame and disrepute that the present issue has brought upon the line. The luminescence of their ancient "gloire" (v. 57) serves only to shed light on its present dullness.

Recurrent allusions to slothfulness (v. 60; cf. v. 20), the repeated image of superposition ("Envain vous vous couvrez des vertus de vos Peres" [v. 61; cf. vv. 7, 30, 44]), and accusations of emptiness (doubly empty because illusory: "vaines chimeres" [v. 62; cf. vv. 1, 6, 38]) lead the speaker to a cacophony of personal abuse heaped upon the listless, hollow, amorphous, dull, motionless, and ultimately perfidious "Fat." In *Satire IV* the Pedant, Bigot, Gambler, Spendthrift, and their fellow fools were not subjected to these insults. In this case, however, such outrageous name-calling (vv. 63–65) appears justified inasmuch as the idea of nobility is vitally important as a model to be emulated by the rest of society. Although the other examples of human folly are far from benign, the false noble is especially insidious in a society in which a system of inherited privilege provides the paramount organizing principle. This arrangement demands that the present nobles—who should be the present, and thus palpable, exemplars of right behavior—maintain the standards that their forebears instituted. Just as the rotten branch imperils the flourishing tree (v. 66), the cowardly traitor will destroy his family, and eventually the body politic itself. Nature continues to figure prominently in the speaker's formulations: the fauna metaphor of the racehorse shifts to flora with the well-used plant analogy. Aristocrats such as the admirable

Dangeau thus take on essential value, for their purpose as models to be imitated is of critical importance.

The subsequent section of the poem utilizes a device found in *Satires I* (vv. 136–38) and *III* (v. 14), when the speaker, in a paroxysm of rage, must pause to catch his breath. The mollifying "Je m'emporte peut-estre" (v. 67), his admission that his muse has *possibly* injected "trop de fiel et d'aigreur" (v. 68) into his discourse, and his apparently resolute and judicious attempt to calm himself ("Hé bien, je m'adoucis" [v. 70]) misdirect the reader. Although the speaker's tone has changed from overt hostility to composed circumspection, his concessive discussion of the antiquity of the bogus noble's lineage leads to an egregious and offensive slur on the virtue of one of the noble's maternal forebears (his mother, perhaps?)! His mordant sarcasm ("vos Ayeules fideles" [v. 77]) casts doubt on the very source of the target's presumption and pride, since nobility was officially sanctioned only among legitimate offspring. An image of movement again attends the concept of hereditary *préséance*. Harking back to the horse race premise, the family's history is encompassed in "ce long *cercle* d'ans" (v. 76; my emphasis), and "le *cours* de vos ayeux" (v. 80) may have been ingloriously sidetracked in its progress toward the present. The speaker's remarks center on the discrepancy between written evidence of noble descent, which is, after all, meaningless (what does "deux fois seize quartiers" [v. 72] actually *signify?*), and the oftentimes suppressed vagaries of real life. As his definition made clear, present deeds, whether positive or negative, supersede the enigmatic past. The speaker's ironic labeling of each generation of the Fat's ancestry as the assumed "victim" of yet another "Lucrece" episode (v. 82, an explicit allusion to the infamous rape of the noble Lucretia, who killed herself after her disgrace, unlike the women in the Fat's family) seals his contempt.

Aristocracy depends for its existence upon a documented history of signal individual contributions to the collective wellbeing. This account of the past may be fraudulent, as is likely in the case of the Fat. In the next portion of the work the speaker supplies his personal version of this history, an abbreviated retracing of the formation, rise, and fall of the idea of nobility in human society. His interpretation affirms the primal legitimacy of the concept, then elucidates its degradation in the present.

In vv. 83–90 the speaker explains with appropriate nostalgia the original purity and childlike innocence of humanity in antiquity.[23] In this imaginary bygone age of equality and justice, an era in which personal merit alone distinguished noble from commoner, unadorned virtue ("Un Heros de soi-mesme empruntoit tout son lustre" [v. 90]) was supplanted by lies, weak character in need of propping up (vv. 93, 105), meaningless words (vv. 94, 96–101), and delusions (v. 97)—features that echo poetic figures prominent in the speaker's opening indictment (vv. 5–24). Elements closely associated with inferiority in *Satire III*—massive and disordered heaps, language serving to conceal vacuousness rather than expose it, reversal of accepted values—find equally top billing in vv. 91–110. Obfuscation is all. The present science of noble heraldry assembles a formless amalgam of nonsense syllables to designate equally meaningless pictorial symbols for the purpose of assigning qualities that were once plainly visible. The possible pun on the name of the author of several volumes on coats of arms, "Segond" (v. 102), accentuates the second-rate aristocracy that hides behind such empty symbols.[24] What was once first-rate quality must disguise its secondary status with ostentatious display: "luxe" (v. 106), "superbe palais" (v. 107), "valets" (v. 108), "pompeux équipages" (v. 109), and "Pages" (v. 110). The concept of fraudulent substitution summarizes the methods of present-day traffickers of counterfeit nobility. They are like actors, concealing their poor performances within elaborate and fabulously expensive stage settings.

The inevitable next stage (vv. 111–30) in the nobility's evolution centers on money, that most bourgeois of values. Notorious deadbeats whose "quality" exempts them from repaying loans, false nobles, to maintain their stage props and thus avoid total ruin, have discovered the expedient of allying themselves with the "Faquin" (v. 118). The venerable institution of aristocracy, whose majestic embodiment is the King himself, has been betrayed, peddled to the highest bidder. The paradox of this state of affairs does not escape the bitterly ironical speaker, for the Fat has reclaimed "son honneur à force d'infamie" (v. 122).

Associative thought processes lead the speaker to dwell upon the primacy of money in a corrupt society. Everything is for sale, and financial success has become the means to nobility, thus "quality." The very foundation of hereditary prerogative, an accurate historical record, will be falsified for lucre. Dastardly scoundrels like d'Hozier of v. 130 stand ready to create a fictitious account of the rich man's genealogy. In such an anarchic moral environment—which perverts its illustrious history (vv. 11, 14, 18) in the name of virtue—the ancient and once steadfast underpinnings of society are in danger of collapse. The false has supplanted the real. Man, lost within a moral chaos, enslaved by his folly, must have before him a compass guiding him to the real. He desperately requires a model, an example upon which to pattern his own values and behavior.

Accordingly, in the poem's concluding section the speaker returns to his initial addressee, the exemplary Dangeau. Called on by the King to fulfill certain royal expectations, Dangeau has succeeded in avoiding the pitfalls so vigorously recounted in the speaker's history of the rise and fall of the upper class ("Des écueils de la Cour as sauvé ta vertu" [v. 132]). Not surprisingly, the King—this most kingly of kings (v. 136)—emerges as the touchstone of distinguished comportment. Although wreathed in symbols ("l'éclat de lis" [v. 135]; "la pourpre" [v. 136]), this prince shows to the world that his essence coincides with his existence.[25] The word "soi" (v. 135; v. 139, where it rhymes with "Roi") embodies the King's glory, just as the antique hero ("Un Heros de soi-mesme empruntoit tout son lustre" [v. 90]) relied solely on himself, not useless embellishments, to produce the light radiating from his person. As the fount from which all worldly noble perfection flows, Louis XIV stands just beneath God Himself in the enormous hierarchical chain of mankind. Just as Christ calls upon his Elect to serve God, so does the King call upon Dangeau to imitate his royal example, serve him with manifest deeds, and thus secure his everlasting esteem and gratitude.[26] The King's regard will authenticate Dangeau's nobleness, since the royal person, alone among mortals, is the *sine qua non* of honor and virtue.

The crime of the phony noble turns out to be far more pernicious than the follies of the Pedant, the Gambler, the *faux dévot,* and others, decried in the preceding *Satire IV.* Although eminently worthy of our disdain, these fools benefit from the speaker's modest forbearance at the close of the poem. The opposite applies to the fool whose mania for nobility saps the very foundation of contemporary society. By providing dismal present-day examples of an ancient object of reverence, the Fat will incite disrespect, disloyalty, and, eventually, insurrection among a populace that requires and demands the highest standards of comportment from its upper classes, as dictated by their illustrious history. Like the misdeeds of the traitorous poetasters who threaten the King's reputation in the *Discours au Roy* (vv. 21 ff.), the false noble's actions are no less a crime of lèse-majesté. The speaker's dogged entreaty to Dangeau in the poem's final two verses—to demonstrate to others his emulation of the King (". . . et fais voir qu'aujourd'hui / Ton Prince a des Sujets qui sont dignes de lui" [vv. 143–44])—underscores the magnitude of Dangeau's role.

Although not explicitly stated here, the satirical poet, who draws attention to such serious abuses of the body politic, takes on critical importance in a state and society in which the power of example governs all aspects of life. As a representative of his own literary class, the speaker must model his own life and work on the "nobles" within this caste, ancient and modern predecessors who embody "quality" in the poetry of satire. The speaker returns specifically to this subject in *Satires VII* and *IX.* The ensuing *Satire VI,* however, centers on yet another obstruction on the road that leads to his own self-fulfillment, this "trace oû marchoient ses ayeux" (v. 4). This barrier is none other than Damon's bugaboo, the city of Paris, that necessary evil in the life of the speaker, without which his muse would fall mute.

Chapter Five

Looking for Lodging

While *Satire V* focuses on the domain of the aristocrat, *la Cour,* the following poem shifts our attention to *la Ville.*[1] Although presided over by the godlike, exemplary King, the court is a perilous environment, full of fraudulent nobles who defile the glorious tradition of France's distinguished families. In *Satire VI* the speaker directs his satirical gaze toward the *ville,* where he sees yet another dangerous locale, replete with obstacles that threaten to distract and eventually overthrow the contemplative person who attempts to penetrate the veils obscuring human folly. On the associative level, the concept of locale establishes a dialectical link between *Satires V* and *VI.* As a human creation, Paris offers rich inspiration to the satirist poet (cf. *Satire I*), yet has the power to disrupt and destroy his creativity. Boileau will return to the leitmotif of the corrupt city in *Satire VIII.*

Satire VI is a monologue in which the speaker recounts his inability to sleep or to move about, his numerous brushes with death, his alienation, within a twenty-four hour period. The disgruntled speaker concludes his list of woes with bitter reflections on his miserable existence as contrasted with the comfort of the rich, who can buy rest, security, and calm in a noisy, dangerous, unsightly, and corrupt Paris.

Traditionally dubbed *l'embarras de Paris,* the poem imitates structural elements common in Latin formal verse satire. Like Juvenal's *Satire III,* the piece shares elements of the Bionean diatribe, i.e., sharp in tone, informal, conversational, employing personal anecdotes, while implicitly addressing an imaginary second party.[2] Boileau employs many Juvenalian themes—the threat of fire and the subsequent pulling down of houses (v. 7 and vv. 193 ff. in Juvenal; vv. 104 ff. in Boileau); the notion that only the rich can sleep in the city (vv. 232–35 in Juvenal;

vv. 116–24 in Boileau); the filth, dangerous traffic, and noise of the city streets, especially the noise as an impediment to sleep (vv. 235–61 in Juvenal; vv. 17–26 and vv. 30 ff. in Boileau); and the ubiquity of nocturnal thieves and murderers in the city (vv. 278 ff. in Juvenal; vv. 87 ff. in Boileau). In Boileau's poem, these images converge to form a thematic structure wholly different from that of Juvenal's piece. Whereas Juvenal's vituperative speaker attacks the corruption of Roman society and the influx of foreigners while lamenting the passing of the good old days (reminiscent of Damon in *Satire I*), Boileau's speaker focuses on Paris as an obstacle to his creative powers.[3] Juvenal's poem, while undoubtedly supplying some of the themes upon which the French poem's metaphors are based, does not match the metaphorical complexity and coherence of Boileau's poem. The Latin poem presents the complaints of a Roman eager to leave a corrupt, superficial, and dangerous society. The poem's language centers on surface effect: the trappings of the rich, the hypocrisy of the hated Greeks, and the affected poverty of numerous social climbers. Images of penetration and immobility, which form the metaphorical fabric of Boileau's poem, are not used systematically in Juvenal.

In the first section of the poem (vv. 1–14), the speaker describes the lugubrious nocturnal discord that renders sleep impossible:

> Qui frappe l'air, bon Dieu! de ces lugubres cris?
> Est-ce donc pour veiller qu'on se couche à Paris?
> Et quel fâcheux Demon durant les nuits entieres,
> Rassemble ici les chats de toutes les goutieres?
> J'ai beau sauter du lit plein de trouble et d'effroi,
> Je pense qu'avec eux tout l'Enfer est chez moi.
>
> (vv. 1–6)

Sleep, as symbol of literal and figurative regeneration, representing one of the fundamental acts of life, offers a sharp contrast to the speaker's unnatural assailants: he refers to the "fâcheux Demon" (v. 3), "chats" (v. 4, traditional symbols of the mysterious and the supernatural), and "l'Enfer" (v. 6), all of which, apparently, have joined forces to bedevil their hapless victim. The poem's second word, "frappe," suggests that the speaker, in a helpless prone position, is the object of a physical attack. In the mind of the speaker, the nocturnal cacophony has taken on a physical presence and has penetrated the walls of his lodging (v. 6). The external attack represents an allied effort: traditional enemies—cats and mice (". . . Les souris et les rats / Semblent, pour m'éveiller, s'entendre avec les chats" [vv. 9–10])—have banded together to strike at the prostrate speaker.

A kind of threshold imagery appears in this introductory section. Traditionally, sleep has been thought of as a median between two contrasting states: known/unknown, light/shadow, real/imaginary. The outside disturbances prevent the speaker from crossing this portal: they erect an almost palpable barrier to his passage from one state to another. Whereas the speaker is thus "imprisoned" in his bed, his attackers have great freedom of movement, capable of penetrating his private sanctuary (v. 6). The total situation recalls Saint-Amant's caprice, "Le Mauvais Logement." In both poems the helpless, prone, and isolated speaker is the subject of a supernatural attack accompanied by recurrent images of penetration, obstruction, and immobility. The similarity in metaphorical structure between Boileau's satire and Saint-Amant's "Le Mauvais Logement" strongly suggests that Boileau adopted certain Juvenalian themes and combined them with major elements of the metaphorical structure of Saint-Amant's poem. It is clear that Boileau was familiar with the older poet's work and that he was an object of Boileau's critical scorn (see especially *Satire I,* vv. 97–108). This situation creates an interesting historical paradox: Boileau, the hostile critic, apparently borrowed his victim's metaphorical structures in "Le Mauvais Logement" to rejuvenate the Latin themes. Boileau thus drew from ancient as well as modern sources to create *l'embarras de Paris.*[4]

The opening of the piece ends resumptively in vv. 13–14. The speaker laments that he is subject to a crescendo of *malheurs:* "Tout conspire à la fois à troubler mon repos: / Et je me plains ici du moindre de mes maux." Each new torment aggravates a rapidly deteriorating predicament: his nocturnal woes lead to a series of daytime harassments.[5] The poem thus possesses a temporal structure generated by a normal chronological sequence of actions and reactions.[6] In the second part (vv. 15–26), the speaker continues to be the object of attack. The animal sounds of the night gradually yield to an onslaught of human sounds. The speaker once again transforms these noises, investing them with funereal and supernatural overtones (the first human invader is a locksmith who has been summoned by "le Ciel en couroux" [v. 17]; he pounds a "fer maudit" [v. 19]; the church bells clang out a "funebre concert" [v. 24]). Threshold imagery, associated with images of penetration and obstruction, continues in the second section. Significantly, a locksmith produces devices that will act as obstacles:

> . . . un affreux Serrurier, que le Ciel en couroux
> A fait, pour mes pechez, trop voisin de chez nous,
> Avec un fer maudit, qu'à grand bruit il appreste,
> De cent coups de marteau me va fendre la teste.
> (vv. 17–20)

His noise appropriately imitates his product in that both become barriers: his locks bar intruders while his din bars the speaker's passage from wakefulness to sleep. While the speaker remains inside, "restricted" by a series of barriers, the external world is characterized by noise, bustle, and freedom of movement: "J'entens déjà par tout les charettes courir, / Les massons travailler, les boutiques s'ouvrir" (vv. 21–22).

In the longer third section, comprising vv. 27–82, the speaker emerges from his lodging to confront the new day and his enemies directly. A transition similar to the first (vv. 13–14) links the second section to the third: the speaker complains that his plight worsens as the day proceeds (vv. 27–30). At first, the speaker opens an assault upon his assembled adversaries; he *penetrates* a dehumanized throng that deters his freedom of movement: "En quelque endroit que j'aille, il faut fendre la presse / D'un peuple d'importuns qui fourmillent sans cesse" (vv. 31–32). This initial and limited success provokes a counterattack: "L'un me heurte d'un ais, dont je suis tout froissé: / Je vois d'un autre coup mon chappeau renversé" (vv. 33–34). The nonphysical, strident attack (though described in physical terms) of the first two sections has become a concrete act of aggression. The otherworld again intervenes in this melee. The speaker observes the "funebre ordonnance" (v. 35) of a funeral cortege and "une croix de funeste présage" (v. 40) that warn him of the very real perils that he may encounter in the crowded streets of Paris. The speaker is denied freedom of passage—as he was when isolated in his bed chamber. Now a wide variety of obstacles bars his way. Accompanying a colossal traffic jam is a cacophony of barking dogs, lowing cattle, braying jackasses, and swearing citizens that complete the parallel with the previous night's frustrations.

The speaker's perilous escape ("Je me mets au hazard de me faire roüer" [v. 66]) subjects him to the shoving, jabbing crowd as well as to a muddy drenching administered by a certain Guenaud, a well-known contemporary doctor who, "en passant" (v. 68), miraculously appears to enjoy an unrestricted mobility denied the hapless and unprosperous speaker. The affluent Guenaud ("sur son cheval" [v. 68]) prefigures the rich man, who has the power to build as well as destroy all barriers (vv. 119 ff.). The speaker's sole means of escape from a drenching rain is "Un ais sur deux pavez [qui] forme un étroit passage" (v. 76). The "pont chancelant" (v. 78) provides a transition, as it were, from immobility to relative freedom of movement, allowing the speaker to make his way home in a darkening and even more dangerous Paris ("La frayeur de la nuit précipite mes pas" [v. 82]). Once again, threshold imagery comes to the fore here: the plank is a temporary and unsteady bridge between two different states, just as sleep (first section) spans two domains. Images of penetration and obstruction, in concert with threshold imagery, continue to figure prominently in the poem's structure.

In the fourth section (vv. 83–118) the speaker describes his harrowing walk home, and his unsuccessful attempts at sleep. As in daylight, Paris at night is a city of barriers;[7]

> Car si-tost que du soir les ombres pacifiques
> D'un double cadenas font fermer les boutiques,
> Que retiré chez lui le paisible marchand
> Va revoir ses billets et compter son argent.
>
> (vv. 83–86)

While the merchant counts the day's receipts, protected from danger behind impenetrable doors, the speaker must contend with the thieves and murderers who "s'emparent de la ville" (v. 88) after nightfall: "Le bois le plus funeste et le moins frequenté, / Est, au prix de Paris, un lieu de seureté" (vv. 89–90). Once in his room, the speaker's vulnerability to attack, his lack of any protective barrier, is reinforced by his inability to "*fermer* la paupiere" (v. 100; my emphasis) and thus erect any obstacle, however frail, between himself and the outside world. As in the first part, the external world invades the speaker's retreat: "Des Filoux effrontez, d'un coup de pistolet, / Ebranlent ma fenestre, et percent mon vôlet" (vv. 101–02). Forced by fire to leave the partial safety of his lodging, the speaker must reenter the fantastic, almost mythic outdoors:

> J'entens crier par tout: "Au meurtre, on m'assassine";
> Ou: "Le feu vient de prendre à la maison voisine."
> Tremblant et demi mort je me leve à ce bruit,
> Et souvent sans pourpoint je cours toute la nuit.
> Car le feu, dont la flâme en ondes se déploye,
> Fait de nostre quartier une seconde Troye;
> Où maint Grec affamé, maint avide Argien,
> Au travers des charbons va piller le Troyen.
>
> (vv. 103–10)

In contrast to his daytime experience, the speaker now has, ironically, great freedom of movement (v. 106) precisely when he would prefer to enjoy another kind of freedom: to sleep, to cross a threshold that remains impassable. As day breaks, our harried speaker returns to his room: however, "Je fais pour reposer un effort inutile" (v. 115). The new day will, of course, in an endless cycle, bring with it the noise and traffic of the preceding one (vv. 15–24). Verses 116–18 of the fourth section provide a transition to the poem's conclusion. The speaker reflects bitterly that only the man of wealth is able to sleep in Paris, since he has the means to erect barriers between himself and the teeming, noisy streets:

> Ce n'est qu'à prix d'argent qu'on dort en cette ville,
> Il faudroit dans l'enclos d'un vaste logement,
> Avoir, loin de la ruë un autre appartement.
>
> (vv. 116–18)

The poem's concluding section (vv. 119–26) expands upon the speaker's reflections expressed in vv. 116–18. The rich man, in isolating and thus protecting himself from the city, is able to create an earthly paradise:

> Paris est pour un Riche un païs de Cocagne:
> Sans sortir de la ville, il trouve la compagne:
> Il peut dans son jardin tout peuplé d'arbres verds,
> Receler le printemps au milieu des hyvers,
> Et foulant le parfum de ses plantes fleuries,
> Aller entretenir ses douces rêveries.
>
> (vv. 119–24)

In Paris money obviously confers great powers on those who possess it. The word "rêveries" in v. 124, meaning both creative imaginings and nocturnal dreams, is significant here. On the contextual surface, the speaker would appear to insist on "rêveries" in the sense of dreams, since one of his major complaints is the impossibility of sleeping in Paris. The alternative meaning, creative imaginings, suggests that the speaker is an artist, one who must have (and now lacks) the leisure, calm, and solitude necessary to pursue the fancies of his mind.[8] To consider sleeping in its traditional role as a kind of threshold between the known and the unknown or reality and the imagination is to accentuate the speaker's need and desire for sleep. Reinforcing this interpretation is the rapid reference to "l'abbé de Pure" in v. 12. The speaker's enmity toward de Pure and his powerful need to pursue "douces rêveries," both sleeping and waking, point to his identity as a writer. Brody underlines Boileau's conception of the creative act as an autonomous and privileged activity that demands solitude and peace.[9] In this light, the speaker's problems take on a more serious cast: lack of sleep and leisure thwarts his creativity. From the speaker's point of view Paris is more than an annoyance: it becomes a serious enemy to his creativity and hence his craft. As Borgerhoff declares:

> The whole Boileau includes the critic and the painter of society, but such activities are only peripheral. I said that much of his verse was about itself. I wish now to assert the obvious fact that very much of his verse is implicitly or explicitly about *himself.*[10]

On the thematic level, the poem focuses on man's relationship to the outside, urban world represented by the city of Paris. Highly antagonistic, this world seeks to invade and disrupt man's attempts both mentally and physically to go beyond this domain. The piece's thematics arise from a system of metaphors that are dispersed throughout the text and that lend to the poem a high degree of coherence. Threshold imagery, with associated images of penetration and obstruction, emphasize the speaker's ceaseless frustrations: he is not permitted to pass from one place, or indeed from one state, to another. The outside world joins forces to penetrate the speaker's inner world, his body and his lodgings, while concomitantly establishing obstructions barring his passage to a contrasting area or domain (land of "douces rêveries" [v. 124] and "le printemps au milieu des hyvers" [v. 122]).

Despite profound isolation within a teeming city, the speaker's relationship with the external world remains the center of his meditations in *l'embarras de Paris.* The following *Satire VII* takes a different tack, divulging to the reader a completely personal, solitary exercise in which the speaker's "Esprit" engages his Muse. His reflections appear to originate in and evolve from the issues raised in the preceding poem. The speaker's concern about lodging in the last section of *Satire VI* extends metaphorically to *Satire VII,* where he ponders the problem of literary "residence." His reservations about the genre of satire place him in a situation in which, in artistic terms, he seems to have "ni feu ni lieu" (*VI,* v. 125). Where indeed are his proper literary quarters? Without question the city of Paris provides the finest raw materials for the satirist, but at the same time it raises serious impediments—both physical and, above all, psychological—for the strong-minded, free-speaking individual who is Boileau's speaker.

Seemingly intent on abandoning his invectives against the city of Paris, among other targets, and its threat to his poetic endeavors, the speaker in *Satire VII* comes to realize that gratifying one's "manie" (vv. 5, 42; also *Satire IV,* vv. 30, 105) will overcome and crush other, less powerful, resolutions. The speaker's situation offers a variation of the thoughts expressed in *Satire IV,* which stresses that all men are governed by their personal *folie.* As suggested figuratively in *Satire IV* and literally in *Satire VI,* the image of lodging comes to the fore here. Like other men, the isolated, solitary speaker lodges within the "Petites-Maisons" (*IV,* v. 4) of the mind. In this poem he considers options, whether to relocate within another *maison* or to maintain his current aesthetic address.

Self-assessment and analysis are frequent topics among satirists. Boileau's immediate model for *Satire VII* is Horace, *Satires* II.1, in which the speaker addresses concerns about his role as a satirist to an elderly lawyer, Trebátius.[11] Their debate terminates with the speaker's confidence that his best defense against official reprisal is good poetry. Another conspicuous source is Horace, *Satires* I.4, in which the speaker acknowledges his predecessor Lucilius (vv. 6–13), wonders whether satire can be considered real poetry (vv. 39–48), and speaks of his own obscurity and reluctance to read his work to others (vv. 71–73).[12] In his *Satire X* Régnier's speaker also reflects upon the satirist's procedure and predicament:

> J'ouvre les yeux de l'ame et m'efforce de voir
> Au travers d'un chacun; de l'esprit je m'escrime,
> Puis, dessus le papier, mes caprices je rime
> Dedans une satyre où d'un œil doux amer
> Tout le monde s'y voit et ne s'y sent nommer.
> (vv. 116–20)

Boileau's poem opens with an unconventional entreaty ("Muse, changeons de stile, et quittons la Satire") to the speaker's Muse, source of the poetic impulse and supreme master of the direction that this impulse might take.[13] In this light, the speaker's inappropriately blunt request has little prospect of fulfillment. As is required whenever an underling appeals to a higher authority, justifications and explanations accompany the supplication. Set off by the alliterative [me] in v. 2 ("C'est un méchant métier que celui de médire"), the bite of satire as merely a form of *médisance*—idle gossip, slander—distorts the positive function of the genre. More important to the speaker, however, are the consequences for the slanderer. The speaker's absolute certitude ("il est *toûjours* fatal" [v. 3]) that he who speaks ill of others will reap what he sows, underscores his desire for change. Prompted perhaps by the financial distress implied in *Satire VI* (in which he has "ni feu ni lieu" [v. 125]), the speaker uses the frequent image of rapid movement toward a goal ("Maint Poëte aveuglé d'une telle manie, / En courant à l'honneur, trouve l'ignominie" [vv. 5–6], in opposition to his immobility in the preceding piece) to confess his wish for success as well as his deepest fears. Emphasized by stressed placement in v. 6, the dichotomy "honneur"/"ignominie" (rhyming with its cause: "manie") introduces the play of bipolarities that serves as a structural principle in this poem.[14] Exploited in *Satire VI,* the interaction between inner and outer worlds also plays a key role here. The generalized notion of public "mal" corresponding to private misfortune (v. 4) is apparently reversed in vv. 7–8. Moreover, the poet's innermost "manie" (v. 5), in its quest for audience acclaim, may instead breed public disgrace, not to mention private grief.

The antithetical movement of the speaker's evolving meditation continues with the laughing reader juxtaposed to the weeping author, emphatically positioned in the second hemistiches of vv. 7–8: "Et tel mot, pour avoir réjoüi le Lecteur / A coûté bien souvent des larmes à l'Auteur." Despite his pessimism, the underlying implication of an effective author entertaining his reader subverts the force of the speaker's lament. The conviction of inevitable ruin in v. 3 ("toûjours") has been modified a mere five verses later ("bien souvent" [v. 8]). The speaker's determination to retreat from satire thus weakens even as he develops the opening appeal to his Muse. That Muse may well question the sincerity of the supplicant.

The problem of sincerity directs the speaker's meditation in the remainder of the poem's first section (vv. 1–20). Halfheartedly and comically suggesting phony eulogies as an antidote to his lively satirical poetry,[15] the speaker imagines a genre attractive because of its diametrical opposition to his customary "stile." Such money-driven hypocrisy in a writer, however, wipes out his credentials as a poet. Although such dreadful poetry ("ennuyeux" and "froid" [v. 9]) presents obvious worldly advantages to the cynical author, its fate—dust and worms—belies the *raison d'être* of poetry, to please and to instruct the reader. The unread writer, by definition, is no writer at all, whereas the "Auteur malin" (malevolent or harmful) who paradoxically provokes joy ("qui fait rire" [v. 13]) and who simultaneously challenges the accepted opinions of his audience ("Qu'on blâme en le lisant, et pourtant qu'on veut lire: / Dans ses plaisans accés qui se croit tout permis" [vv. 14–15]) has an engaged following. But that bugaboo, the goal that all satirists strive for—frank opinions that may actually verge on the truth—

disqualifies the speaker for the material success that any normal person desires. In the topsy-turvy world of the speaker, readerless "poetry" triumphs over effective, i.e., *read* poetry. Of course, the poet strives to engage his readers, but does he wish to incite fear and hatred in them? Bipolarities—sincerity/insincerity, enjoyment/loathing, neglect/attention, success/failure—continue to pervade the poem's design.

In v. 21 the speaker's renewed attempt to overcome his insistent Muse ("S'il faut rimer ici rimons quelque loüange" [v. 22]) by composing accolades translates into a vain search for a subject. Although Gordon Pocock believes that Boileau "is sailing very near the wind" (27) by implying that no deserving hero exists, the emphasis in this poem is on the speaker's own inability to find rhymes ("Je ne puis pour loüer rencontrer une rime" [v. 26]), i.e., to persuade his Muse to sustain him in this endeavor. Spontaneity flees when insincerity approaches. Reminiscent of the metaphorical structure of *Satire VI,* images of physical attacks on normally cooperative but now unyielding obstacles ("J'ay beau frotter mon front, j'ay beau mordre mes doigts" [v. 28]) illustrate his struggle to find inspiration. Conversely, the speaker's proclivity for mocking rhymes appears—not unexpectedly—in his description of resistance and restriction. His dig at Chapelain's *La Pucelle* substantiates his contention that derision is his instinctive manner. Sufferings like those highlighted in *Satire II* dissipate whenever Esprit allows the persistent Muse full rein: "Phébus, dés que je parle, est prest à m'exaucer" [v. 35]). Swift, purposeful movement again characterizes the Muse's emancipation.

As is often the case in Boileau, corroborative examples are contained in the speaker's message. The words that ". . . viennent sans peine et courent se placer" (v. 36) take shape immediately before the reader's eyes in the ensuing lines. The type actuates the example/rhyme:

> Faut-il peindre un *fripon fameux* dans cette *Ville?*
> Ma main, sans que j'y rêve, écrira *Raumaville.*

And:

> Faut-il d'un *sot parfait* montrer *l'original?*
> Ma plume au bout du vers d'abord trouve *Sofal.*
> (vv. 37–40; my emphasis)

This illusion of involuntary facility becomes a cascade of scornful abuse when the actuating type ("froid Rimeur" [v. 42]) hails from the literary domain.[16] No less than six examples quickly tumble from the satirist's suddenly prolix pen:

> Mes vers, comme un torrent, coulent sur le papier.
> Je rencontre à la fois Perrin et Pelletier,
> Bonnecorse, Pradon, Colletet, Titreville,
> Et pour un que je veux, j'en trouve plus de mille.
>
> (vv. 43–46)

In accordance with his key assertion in v. 34 ("Alors certes alors, je me connois *Poëte*"; my emphasis), verse rhythms and sonorities, not specifically selected satirical targets, govern the choice of names.[17] Alliteration of [p] (on the accented seventh and tenth syllables of v. 44; including the allied [b] in "Bonnecorse" in the first syllable in v. 45), [k], [r], [t], [l], and assonance in [∈], [i], and [e] provide ample evidence that the speaker is no "froid Rimeur." That "Titreville" rhymes with "mille" (cf. Horace, *Satires* II.1.3–4) plays up the notion of quantity vs. quality so prominent in *Satire III.*

The Muse's smug self-satisfaction stemming from this "beau coup" (v. 48) of creative energy strengthens the speaker's illustrated explanation *cum* justification of his penchant for raillery. Entirely within the mind of the speaker, this "victory" inflates his sense of self-worth and respect. External recognition has nothing to do with the rewards received. Although Raison may intervene by chastising the unrepentant speaker, his mistress Muse refuses to give quarter to his myriad victims. The speaker elaborates on his antipodal opposition to the panegyrist, who is concerned solely with the external rewards of his writing. The external, on the other hand, enters the picture in the form of his confident (but not unshakable, as we shall see) knowledge that readers will indeed read him (vv. 13–14).

The situation described here echoes the role of reason in the last section of *Satire IV:* an ineffectual corrective to the various *manies* that dominate humankind. On returning to the issue, the speaker explores more fully his personal mania, merely suggested in the former poem. The "leçons" (v. 50) that he gives himself correspond to the nagging voice of reason (*Satire IV,*

vv. 115–20), and can have no effect, since his "fureur" (meaning both poetic inspiration and dementia) have co-opted his psyche. Moderation is out of the question. The notorious guard dog metaphor in vv. 57–58[18] underscores the speaker's instinctive, natural, i.e., uncontrollable, tendency to bark whenever he "smells" a Fat. The speaker wisely contends, however, that a rational process precedes his warning yelps. Like an all-inclusive filter (v. 54), his endlessly attentive mind sifts the outer world. The relative scarcity of genuine merit around him is mirrored in v. 55 ("Le Merite pourtant m'est toûjours precieux"), the only verse devoted to this rare phenomenon. The sentiment is almost lost among the more numerous notes of disapproval. The speaker thus insists that he has the capacity to recognize and to praise virtue, despite the pessimistic slant of his perspective.

This fragile bid at self-justification is absorbed in the speaker's modest assessment of his poetic competence in vv. 60–62, which tends to minimize his social impact. Similar to Horace's admission in *Satires* I.4.39–48 (in which he calls his verse *sermo merus* [v. 48], "mere prose talk"[19]), the speaker's humility, like so much else in *Satire VII,* seems to belie other verses in which he is less reticent, v. 34, for example. Indeed, Boileau's real skill produces temptingly quotable, aphoristic verses, which partly explains the fragmentation that his work has so often suffered.[20] The claim that he possesses narrow talents ("Je sçai coudre une rime au bout de quelques mots: / Souvent j'habille en vers une maligne prose" [v. 60]) can be disproved by close analysis of almost randomly chosen verses. Boileau's insistence on *la rime* (cf. *Satire II*) is particularly germane to his comic lines, so dependent on unexpected, perhaps shocking, finales. The end rhyme creates syntactic tension that is released when the rhyme reveals itself. This is a preferred device in Boileau, and can be seen, for example, in vv. 29–30:

> Je ne puis arracher du creux de ma cervelle,
> Que des vers plus forcez que ceux de la Pucelle.

Briefly, additional formal points here include the near rhyme [se]/[ʃe] at the caesura, and the syntactic and phonetic parallelism in the second hemistiches. This device is also used in vv. 36–40.

The ensuing *confiteor* discloses the overweening influence of his satirical Muse:

> Deust ma Muse par là choquer tout l'Univers,
> Riche, gueux, triste ou gay, je veux faire des vers.
> (vv. 67–68)

Directly inspired by Horace, *Satires* II.1.57–60,[21] this unequivocal expression of the speaker's *manie* (his "fureur extrême" [v. 49]) generates the brusque intercession of a third party. Although identified simply as "on" (cf. *Satire I,* v. 100), this clear voice of Raison was anticipated in v. 50. A literal *mise en œuvre* of what the speaker had described just several lines before, the poem presents a brief explication of a device followed by an illustration of that device. This self-reflexive, self-scrutinizing technique, based on the concept of the exemplum, integrates into the basic thematic structure of this poem. The work concretizes the poetic procedures adduced in the speaker's self-analysis.

Raison's interpretation of the cause of Esprit's compulsion is couched in the form of seventeenth-century physiological and psychological beliefs. Apparently relying on contemporary medical knowledge and practice based on the four humors, "Dr." Raison categorizes the speaker's alleged depressive psychological condition—his "melancolie"—in liquid terms:

> «Pauvre Esprit», dira-t-on, «que je plains ta folie.
> Modere ces boüillons de ta melancolie,
> Et garde qu'un de ceux que tu penses blâmer,
> N'éteigne dans ton sang cette ardeur de rimer.»
> (vv. 69–72)

The "boüillons" of his black mental state flow in his blood, which in turn may be spilled if the speaker recklessly persists in his impulsive satirical ways. His intensity is hot—"boüillons," "éteigne," "ardeur"—in marked contrast to the "froid" (vv. 9, 42) associated with lesser poets. This eminently pragmatic advice to cool his ardor relates only to the speaker's position in the external world; it does not, nor can it, change the speaker's "stile," which is ruled by his internal, despotic Muse. The futility of Raison's counsel had of course been predicted in vv. 49–50:

> C'est envain qu'au milieu de ma fureur extrême,
> Je me fais quelquefois des leçons à moi-mesme.

Although dismissed as a "répétition fâcheuse" (Ascoli 97), the seemingly trivial "envain" becomes a leitmotif in the poem, first utilized in emphatic position (v. 21) in an effort to intimidate the Muse, then in each subsequent use (vv. 25, 49, 51) applied to the Muse's actual power in the face of Esprit's hollow bravado, thus enhancing the rhetorical dynamics of the poem.

The speaker's riposte to Raison is a well-devised argument grounded on prior example that demolishes the poetic objective voiced in v. 1. Maintaining the fluid imagery of humors (vv. 74, 78), the speaker immediately cites—quite naturally, since these verses spring directly from Horace, *Satires* II.1.62 ff.—Horace himself, then Lucilius, as worthy satirical precursors. This wink at the reader establishes a kind of satirical genealogy in which literary progenitors not only provide the raw material from which to create new poems, but also furnish career prototypes from which their descendants might draw encouragement and reassurance in their own vocations.[22] Like the present-day speaker, such celebrated antecedents possessed the magical ability to transform insubstantial, ephemeral "vapeurs" (v. 74) and "flots" (v. 78) into "bons mots" (literally, *good words*): concrete expressions of outraged virtue (v. 75).[23] This interaction of abstract and concrete, inner and outer, converges in Juvenal's "mordante plume" (v. 77): the pen's snapping jaws—recapitulating the barking guard dog metaphor—actualize the poet's black bile, which in turn materializes in the ink of the satirists' "traits éclatans" (*traits* meaning "barbs" and "writing" [v. 75]). Despite their righteous anger and courage in the face of countless antagonists—Juvenal railed at "tout le peuple Latin" (v. 79)—the speaker contends that this satirical triad did not meet untimely death at the hands of their enemies.[24]

Whatever the real-life fate reserved for his illustrious predecessors, the speaker ultimately takes refuge in his own present obscurity. This rationalization represents a complete turnabout from his initial resolve to abandon satire. His declaration that "Personne ne connoist ni mon nom ni ma veine" (v. 82), while appearing to insulate him from the dangers of the outside world, contradicts the theme of an engaged audience for the "Auteur malin" in vv. 13–15. Furthermore, that the speaker is not yet published (vv. 83–84) certainly does not mean that he is unknown among his contemporaries, since his poetry has been exposed to public scrutiny at private readings. Given the nature of his work, publication is not essential: oral diffusion alone would promote the unknown poet's name.[25] In choosing to write satire and, more importantly, to promulgate it ("A peine quelquefois je me force à les lire, / Pour plaire à quelque Ami que charme la satire" [vv. 85–86]), the speaker has in fact made a clear choice between silence and speech, risk and security, isolation and engagement.

This decision places the speaker in a sphere wherein his own poetic sincerity magnifies his doubt as to the sincerity of those around him. In vv. 87–88 he reiterates the hypocritical reactions (cf. vv. 15–16) of his "approving" audience:[26] "Qui me flatte peut-estre, et d'un air imposteur, / Rit tout haut de l'ouvrage, et tout bas de l'Auteur." This return to the satirist's ambiguous position—he may weep while his readers laugh (vv. 7–8)—once again features bipolar images. The horizontal inner-outer dynamic of his public reading of private invention intersects with the verticality of the outer "high" and inner "low" laughter of the so-called friend. In his defensive response to Reason in vv. 73–88, the speaker's convoluted dialectical reasonings—satire is dangerous: but not for his famous forebears; he is unknown: his public ridicules him—finally come back to the one true explanation for his persistence in the genre of satire.[27] In spite of the enigmatic and treacherous outside world, the yearning for inner contentment drives the speaker. Moreover, resistance to his omnipotent Muse is futile; she is a force of nature, an unstoppable "torrent" (v. 93). The speaker's hopeless and insincere attempts to change his "stile" ends in the not unexpected realization that nature cannot be changed. The poem's final three verses renew and solidify the bonds of intuitive understanding between the Muse and Esprit. The return to inclusive imperative extends an invitation to the Muse to recognize the speaker's mortal limitations (the metonymic "main"—exhausted in v. 95—eagerly "itchy" in v. 21). The partnership bringing together the inspirational Muse, the subordinate Esprit (who supplies the will), and the physical "main" (the slavish manual laborer) can easily overwhelm Reason's arguments to cease and desist. Fatigue will temporarily stay the Muse, but the future holds ever renewed rebeginnings.

Satire VII itself constitutes a transcribed, therefore tangible, object that replicates the speaker's inner struggle. References to oral performance (vv. 85, 90, 94)—i.e., intangible, fleeting re-creations of the speaker's inner life—interact with the permanent inscription of these communications (vv. 83, 92, 95), which of course exists as Boileau's *Satire VII.* This appeal to his Muse, presented simultaneously as an oral discourse and a written artifact ("C'est assez parlé. Prenons un peu d'haleine. / Ma main, pour cette fois, commence à se lasser" [vv. 94–95]), incorporates the antithetical elements of the material versus the immaterial, of the enduring versus the ephemeral. The speaker's mention of past satirical geniuses, in contrast to his alleged present anonymity, parallels this transience-permanence dichotomy.[28] For this reason his determination to recommence "demain" (v. 96) in the poem's emphatic concluding line reinforces his awareness of the relationship to his literary mentors and of the true nature of the poetic enterprise. He is, after all, not writing for the falsely flattering friend, just as Juvenal, in the end, did not write for "tout le peuple Latin" (v. 79). Juvenal's intended audience transcended mere temporal or geographical boundaries. The "tragique fin" (v. 80) never encountered by Lucilius, Horace, or Juvenal thus takes on figurative resonances. It is reserved for the "froid Rimeur" (v. 42) and his "éloge ennuyeux" (v. 9), unread in his own lifetime and for generations to come. Given these stakes, Reason's feeble revolt was clearly doomed from the outset.

Boileau's self-assessment and analysis recognizes that his own *folie* resides in his zealous quest for dullness and his need to speak out (write) against it. His insistence on the ongoing nature of this process in the last three verses assures an endless cycle: he can no more forsake satire than the various types lampooned in *Satire IV* can repudiate their respective fixations. The speaker cites his own case as an example of the theme of universal folly among men. The ensuing *Satire VIII* takes up the allied question of the role of reason as potential corrective to pervasive madness.

The more philosophically oriented *Satire VIII* offers the reader a sequel to its predecessor.[29] It is a "rebeginning" (*VII,* v. 96), in the sense that it delves into the very foundation of what defines a human being as human, sole earthly creature endowed with reason, measure of all things, master of the world. At the end of *Satire VII* the speaker's resolution to continue the practice of satire, and thus to renounce the timid and apprehensive voice of Raison in its efforts to suppress and silence his Muse, results in his decision to put humanity and reason on trial. *Satire VIII* pursues the indictment of human reason vs. instinct launched in *Satire VII,* in an effort to inculpate the force for rebellion in the speaker's psyche. Aside from its doctrinal perils, the speaker's paradoxical position concerning man's relative status extends the notion embodied in *Satire VII* that an instinctive predisposition to certain thoughts and behaviors transcends the dictates of reason. Reason in itself does not imply wisdom. On the contrary, instinct, obedience to nature, provides an infallible guide on the road to wisdom.

Contrary to our customary view of the legendary Boileau as that relentless defender of classical precepts and adversary of the preceding generation, the poet patterns the initial development of his *Satire VIII* on Théophile de Viau's *Satire I.* The influence of *libertinage* on Boileau has been noted in his indictment of reason and in his contention that folly is universal among men in *Satire IV.* Like Boileau, Théophile cites the smitten lover, the grasping merchant, the seeker of military glory, the nobility hound, and the rich miser as signal examples of man's irrational nature. The infamous *libertin*'s fundamental message, that God, Soul, Reason, and Free Will—officially looked upon as philosophical first principles—have scant relevance in the confused tableau of everyday experiences, can be inferred in *Satire VIII.* In its view of man's multifarious and erratic passions, his lack of will and of real knowledge, Boileau's poem mimics Théophile's Epicurean belief that Nature, and not an omnipotent rational Intelligence, governs the world.[30] The implications of Théophile's defiant concluding lines remain unspoken in Boileau:

> Je pense que chacun auroit assez d'esprit,
> Suivant le libre train que Nature prescrit.
> A qui ne sçait farder, ny le cœur, ny la face,
> L'impertinence mesme a souvent bonne grace:
> Qui suivra son Genie, et gardera sa foy,
> Pour vivre bien-heureux, il vivra comme moy.[31]

His satirical intent in *Satire VIII* nonetheless seems clear. Théophile's conclusion might be taken as an affirmation of the speaker's final resolution of *Satire VII* and the motive behind his condemnation of reason in its successor.

The introverted meditation that is *Satire VII* switches to a wide-ranging, public debate with *M***, Docteur de Sorbonne,* eminently qualified to refute the speaker's assertions. Succinctly stated in the first four verses, his thesis introduces an almost literal boundless confidence in the accuracy of his statement:

> De tous les Animaux qui s'élevent dans l'air,
> Qui marchent sur la terre, ou nagent dans la mer,
> De Paris au Perou, du Japon jusqu'à Rome,
> Le plus sot animal, à mon avis, c'est l'Homme.

Embracing three of the four elements accepted in contemporary science, the speaker takes care to include the natural habitats of all known living beasts,[32] then embellishes the cosmological-biological scope of vv. 1–4 with a geographical amplification that poetically embraces the known world. Verses 1–2 inject a biblical flavor, specifically a passage from the Creation in Genesis 1.26:

> And God said, Let us make man in our image, after our likeness: and let them have dominion over the fish of the sea, and over the fowl of the air, and over the cattle, and over all the earth, and over every creeping thing that creepeth upon the earth.

The speaker's burlesque reversal of God's solemn injunction boldly sets the tone for a poem in which man's "divine" preeminence will be systematically debased. Man's superlative folly, not his superiority as the sole creature created in the image of God, emerges as the comic proof of his claim to exclusive "dominion."

The poem's initial rhyme "air"/"mer" evokes a vertical all-inclusiveness that accompanies the enormous horizontal range of the alliterative v. 3: "De Paris au Perou, du Japon jusqu'à Rome." The spatial expanse supposedly emblematic of man's intellectual and moral superiority is inverted in the reaction of the orthodox *on* in vv. 5–8. Introduced in emphatic position in

v. 5, the ant anticipates the proverbial account of its exemplary wisdom in vv. 25–34.[33] In abruptly compressing the expansive introductory images, the tiny "ver" and "fourmi" initiate a pattern of images of expansion and contraction, or, indeed, of inflation and deflation, that underlie the poem's metaphorical structure. The speaker's contention that the physically and intellectually minuscule "insect rampant" (again echoing the Bible) is "mieux tourné" (i.e., better "designed") than man reverses the divinely sanctioned pretensions suggested in vv. 1–3. The syntactically parallel "taureau qui rumine" and the "chevre qui broute"—the well-known beasts of the field—in v. 7 further reinforce the biblical slant of the poem's opening lines. The speaker presents a topsy-turvy thesis in which "down" (the lowly creeping insect, the grazing—heads turned downward—cattle and goats) becomes "up" (morally superior), and "up" (man) becomes "down" (below an ant).

The speaker's beast-over-man premise elicits the expected reaction of shock and opposition from the poem's addressee. Representing an institution in which belief in man's dominant cosmological position forms the very foundation of theology, this Sorbonne doctor naturally mouths the official dogma in vv. 10–12. The professor's all-embracing statement ("Bois, prez, champs, animaux, tout est pour son usage" [v. 11]) rebroadens the scope of the argument. Not unexpectedly, the doctor's insinuation that man's unique reason is the touchstone of his supremacy receives the speaker's partial agreement. Indeed, man's reason distinguishes him from the rest of nature, but as "le plus sot" (v. 14; repeated from v. 4), and not as "le chef et le Roy" (v. 10). The professor's attempt to denigrate the speaker's general proposition, to reduce it to the paltry realm of satire,[34] prompts the clever speaker to exalt his lowly "satirical" arguments to the level of a fusty academic colloquy: "Répons-moi donc, Docteur, et mets-toi sur les bancs" (v. 18). In placing the professor among the students, "sur les bancs," the speaker has succeeded in reversing the roles of expert and neophyte inherent in the student-professor relationship.

Of course, the effort to indict reason relies on logical, or at least logically appearing, argument, a paradox universally exploited among praisers of folly.[35] The speaker's first question ("Qu'est-ce que la Sagesse?" [v. 19]) and sketchy answer, a definition of wisdom derived essentially from the Stoic concept of ataraxia, carries the notion of rhythmic, modulated movement toward an elevated goal ("Qu'un Doyen au Palais ne monte les degrez" [v. 22]). Although the "Doyen" strives to simulate *gravitas* in his movements,[36] appearance and reality actually coincide in the hoary example of the ant.[37] Again, juxtaposed images of expansion and contraction underpin the speaker's discourse. The puffed-up figure of the ermine-berobed judge (cf. v. 172), common in satirical literature,[38] yields to the Aesopic ant as a more fitting model for wisdom. The ant's insignificant size notwithstanding, it is restricted neither spatially nor temporally; the ant in effect bestrides the earth year after year ("La Fourmi *tous les ans traversant* les guerets" [v. 25; my emphasis]), storing treasures that stretch far beyond the confines suggested by its diminutive physical stature. Dramatically unlike the human miser treated later in the poem, the ant's useful hoarding ("tresors de Cerés" [v. 26]) allows it to overcome the dictates of nature while still obeying its laws. By living within nature, the lowly ant reveals to man that a modulated, rhythmic pattern of life can "conquer" (v. 30) the vagaries of nature. The secret is self-knowledge and consequent adaptation to one's natural makeup. Marked allusions to the year's changing seasons, months, and the cyclical return of the signs of the zodiac (vv. 30–34) underscore the necessity of finding one's niche in the cosmic scheme.

The "retour de Belier" in v. 34, conjuring up spring, season of warmth, fertility, renewal, and, above all, love—all that is positive in the natural world—reinforces the dialectical transition to man in vv. 35–54, who incarnates the opposite. Out of step with this world, mankind signifies incessant, unregulated motion, indeterminate directions and desires, and unfocused, unstable love. The portrait of the newly married Marquis exemplifies the fool in love, who extravagantly believes that God has re-created womanhood just for him (vv. 47–48). Man's expansive self-image—his fantasy that natural laws (e.g., woman's infidelity!) can be nullified in the name of his personal happiness—contradicts his actual *petitesse.* Reference to the passing months—zodiacal units—and the speaker's mention of the "saints" of cuckoldry in a contemporary satirical *livre d'heures* (v. 42)[39] reinforce the disparity between mercurial man and undeviating nature revealed in the cyclical motion of the zodiac and the regular progress of time as measured by the calendar and the clock (vv. 44, 45, 50, 54). Man's insouciant attitude toward the mandates of nature and the divine simply demonstrates his confidence that he is superior to the world around him. This enables him to remain ignorant of his inner being: to don a soldier's helmet one day, a priest's habit the next (v. 54).

The speaker's ironical commentary on man's vacuous presumption in vv. 55–59 insists on his antithetical nature. Man is termed doubly "light-headed" ("plein de *vapeurs legeres*" [v. 55; my emphasis], the medical term *vapeurs* indicating a subtle humor that clouds the mind), a description that recalls the sham noble in *Satire V,* vv. 5–24. He is, however, *full* of emptiness, contrary to his belief that he is the rock-solid axis around which the universe revolves. The Sorbonne doctor's persistent self-assurance in v. 60 is greeted by the speaker's equally sure confidence in his own arguments ("«Qui pouroit le nier?» poursuis-tu. Moi peut-estre"). Man's mastery over nature is a foolish delusion: he is not a master lawgiver, but rather the slave to a myriad of irresistible forces. The speaker's allusions to nature's predetermined harmony as manifested in the heavens (vv. 34, 35, 58, for example) valorize the concept of destiny as the controlling factor in man's life.

To pursue his argument, the speaker declares that avarice, ambition, hatred, and love are chief among the forces that enslave man's mind. Accordingly, as we have seen in other poems, precise examples sharpen the point. Taken directly from Persius's *Satire V,* vv. 132 ff., the merchant's compulsion to pursue unneeded wealth is dramatized as allegorical Avarice awakening the reluctant sleeper. Images of contraction and expansion invest the scene. Snatched from the pleasant dreamland within his own head, the merchant must obey Avarice's summons "Pour courir l'Ocean de l'un à l'autre bout" (v. 74). The merchant's attempts to "see" during a voyage to the domain of Morpheus ("Le sommeil sur ses yeux commence à s'épancher" [v. 69]) is grotesquely transformed into a real-life trading voyage enveloping the whole world. Unnatural compulsions can and will obliterate purely natural demands such as sleep. The example of the wise ant contrasts sharply with the merchant's activity. The latter scours the world in order to amass a useless hoard that brings only suffering, whereas the virtuous ant accumulates riches that will ensure its comfort and ultimate survival.[40] The ant's quest for life becomes in man an aberrant urge to live in misery, to stockpile even at the expense of life itself ("De peur de perdre un liard, souffrir qu'on vous égorge" [v. 84]). Avarice's deadpan *reductio ad absurdum* explanation for this behavior in vv. 85–88 further exploits the ironic distinctions between the ant and man:

> —«Et pourquoi cette épargne enfin?» —«L'ignores-tu?
> Afin qu'un Heritier bien nouri, bien vêtu,
> Profitant d'un trésor en tes mains inutile,
> De son train quelque jour embarrasse la ville.»

We hardly need emphasize that the prime motivation for the ant's labor includes its desire for the long-term survival of the race. In obedience to nature's laws, the ant's progeny will imitate it, vastly unlike the miser's ungrateful offspring who, unheedful of future generations, will luxuriate in the treasure that he so painfully accumulated.

The motif of the voyage provides transition from avarice to ambition. In both cases man is snatched from the comforts of home to chase his "dream"—which ironically can be found in his own head, as suggested by the awakened sleeper in vv. 69 ff., and which can equally apply to the one whom ambition likewise awakens (vv. 91–92). As with much else in life, prior example nourishes the unceasing hunt for military glory. While ambition invites the demented victim to become another "César," this expansive, grandiose fantasy will be recounted not in an epic poem, but rather in a perfunctory obituary in the "Gazette," which presumably has the questionable permanence of any newspaper full of *faits divers.* The speaker's burlesque treatment of martial deeds centers on the ultimate exemplum, the great Alexander, who becomes just another *fou,* an "écervelé" whose mania unfortunately was not as innocuous as most men's follies. His craving to "emplir toute la terre" (v. 108) reiterates the territoriality instinct, the desire for possession, that the newlywed and the merchant also exhibited. Psychotically antagonistic to the "obscurité" enjoyed by the wise ant (vv. 29–30), this "Bandit" (v. 106) with a god complex should have been locked within the "petites-Maisons" (v. 110; cf. *Satire IV,* v. 4) to which all men, implicitly, should be restricted. Ranging from the "monde entier" (v. 102) to the tiny holding cells of the asylum, the speaker's account of the "fougueux l'Angely" is organized around images of expansion and contraction.

The speaker's abrupt shift away from Alexander in v. 113 plays on the notions of travel or motion as well as expansion and contraction. His desire to avoid "digressions" from his main topic (from the Latin *digressio,* "a move away from") and not to embrace more than he can rhetorically grasp (he does not wish to describe "toutes les passions" [v. 114]) induces him to contract his ambitiously—no verbal Alexander, he!—expansive treatment of man's follies intimated in vv. 67–68: "L'Ambition, l'Amour, l'Avarice, ou la Haine / Tiennent comme un forçat son esprit à la chaîne." Although he depicts love (vv. 37–48), cupidity (vv. 69–89), and ambition (vv. 90–111), hatred is never equally developed. In the movement of his discourse, he strives to avoid, on the verbal level, the megalomaniacal overreaching ("Dogmatiser en vers et rimer par chapitres" [v. 116]) of the merchant and the military hero that he has just described. His indictment of reason will undergo ebbs and flows in accordance with the dictates of his inspiration (cf. *Satire VII,* vv. 33–36). Consequently, the poem's ongoing developmental structure proceeds in concert with the dominant metaphorical patterns.

The speaker's concern for order, harmony, and coherence (vv. 115–16) quite logically leads to an analysis of "l'endroit le plus beau" in his anatomy of man. Following Aristotle's view that man's political and judicial structures epitomize his intellectual and moral aptitude, Boileau examines "l'*enceinte* des villes" (v. 119; my emphasis), thus further "contracting" his focus. The chief symbolic *locus* of man's achievements as well as the hunting ground of choice for the satirist (see *Satire I*), the city, closed off from so-called savage nature (vv. 128–30), receives perfunctory treatment in vv. 118–22.[41] Man, huddled "dans l'enceinte des villes," has formed tiny sanctuaries of what he terms "civil order" against what he views as nature's lawlessness. In true perspective, however (cf. vv. 1–3), the metropolis resembles the "petites-Maisons" (v. 110) in which human madness reigns. Man's subversion of natural laws has forced him to erect a vast political and judicial apparatus that strives, through the exercise of fear (v. 124), to curb mankind's moral anarchy.

In v. 145 the judge's ludicrous efforts to decree sexual intercourse disclose the burlesque magnitude of man's delusional "mastery" of nature.[42] Like the new husband, the grasping merchant, and the would-be Alexander, man the city dweller, the lawgiver, detached from the benevolent laws of nature, is obliged to replace them with ineffectual substitutes. The speaker's denunciation of civilizations's laws in contrast with natural laws ("les pures loix de la simple équité" [v. 150]) handed down from a benevolent Nature evokes the legendary Golden Age (cf. *Satire V,* vv. 83–90), which still prevails in the animal kingdom. Natural justice ("équité" [vv. 150, 158]) has literally been buried under an excrescence of statutes concocted by generations of ambitious "Docteurs" (v. 157). The image of a huge, amorphous mound ("monceux d'Auteurs" [v. 158]) recalls similar images, especially in *Satires II* and *III* when unchecked profusion further overwhelmed the concept of quality. The city, man's "endroit le plus beau" ironically introduced in v. 118, emerges in this section as the locus and origin of literally countless "harangueurs" (v. 160) whose vital interest is to fabricate and sustain a tangled mass of laws made necessary by man's depravity. Although advertised as the crowning glory of man's reason, his system of jurisprudence provides ample testimony that the opposite is the case.

The *docteur de Sorbonne* takes immediate, no doubt personal, exception to the speaker's wholesale attack on "Docteurs" and their "ennuieuse éloquence" in vv. 157–60. He appears, at least initially, to be a worthy adversary by simultaneously accusing the speaker of intemperate emotions (e.g., lack of "sagesse"; cf. vv. 19–21) and then by using that indignation as an example of human imperfection, man's "passions" (v. 162), and "ses flots et ses caprices" (v. 163). His argument, that man, by literally taking the measure of the universe, has proved himself superior to it, merely repeats the speaker's ironical "L'Homme de la nature est le chef et le Roy" (v. 10) that he had put in the mouth of the Docteur at the beginning of the poem. The notion of measurement—both numerical and otherwise—comes to the fore in this section.

Both speaker and Docteur are, after all, "taking the measure" of man. After his pointed reference to passion as a signal vice, the expansive Docteur speaks in cosmic terms in vv. 165–68, portraying man and his "compas" as a second God, or at least a subject created in His image:

> N'est-ce pas l'Homme enfin, dont l'art audicieux
> Dans le tour d'un compas a mesuré les Cieux?
> Dont la vaste science embrassant toutes choses,
> A foüillé la nature, en a percé les causes?

For the grandiloquent Docteur, the microcosm's discovery of order and harmony (both symbolized by his "compas" [v. 166]) in an outwardly inscrutable macrocosm demonstrates his proximity to God. His enthusiasm, however, leads to his ill-advised, if not unexpected (the university is his bailiwick!) use of another measure of man's alleged primacy, the "quatre Facultez" of Theology, Letters, Law, and Medicine that represent the sum of man's intellectual advances. The speaker seizes this opening, exploiting the satirist's stock contempt for physicians with the customary "Medecin"/"assassin" rhyme in vv. 173–74. In the animal world there is no need for the art and science of medicine: the hearty life in the "bois" (v. 174, implicitly, far from the city's miasmas) permits no human poisons.

The speaker's principal argument centers on the disparity between popular opinion and the Docteur's veneration for the mind's supposed progress as symbolized by the university. The speaker, pragmatic man of the world, sees that wealth is the true measure of man's worth in the contemporary world. The father-son scene in which the younger generation accepts the crucial lesson that money ("vingt livres" [v. 184]) promotes greater success than "tous les livres" (v. 183) reinforces not only the power of mathematics over erudition, but also the notion that such values will carry over from generation to generation. In the modern world, and presumably far into the future, a measurement—simple arithmetic (*not* ". . . l'art audacieux / Dans le tour d'un compas a mesuré les Cieux"! [vv. 165–66])—determines the value of a man.[43] In the ethical chaos of the real world the quantity of the rich man's *livres,* amassed through "cruautez" (v. 196), will attract a crowd (vv. 197–98) of learned mercenaries. These fraudulent agents of *sagesse* will gladly debase virtue and elevate vice ("Dégrader les Heros pour te mettre en leurs places" [v. 199]) if financial gain is involved.[44] The ultimate expansion derives from riches: "Quiconque est riche est tout" (v. 203).

The speaker's *avis au docteur* in vv. 215–30 plays further upon the images of expansion and contraction. The biblical scholar's monumental, life-long labors, encompassing geographical (v. 216), spiritual (v. 217), theological (v. 218), and historical (v. 219) questions, will in the end be enclosed within the leather binding of an unread volume. The burlesque rhyme in vv. 223–24 reveals that the professor's epic achievement ("la Bible éclaircie") will be reduced to three hollow words—"Je vous remercie"—by the "heureux Faquin" who cares not a whit for such unprofitable commodities. In vv. 225–28 the speaker's advice to the Docteur—to become a banker—ironically mimics the father's "wise" counsel to his son.

In the following section of the poem (vv. 231–46), the professor steers the debate back to its initial terms concerning the value of reason as opposed to instinct. The Docteur continues to maintain that man's reason guarantees his primacy. But the "Poëte" (v. 231) insists that the Docteur's "pilote fidele" (v. 235) is blind to any "écueil" (v. 238) that threatens man's voyage through life. The speaker's use of exemplum again concretizes the abstruse arguments that he deploys. A prominent enemy of Boileau, the Abbé Cotin (*Satire III,* v. 60; *IX,* v. 276),[45] cannot heed the voice of Raison exhorting him to renounce his insane desire to be a poet. Outwardly, Cotin's dogged persistence differs little from the speaker's situation in *Satire VII,* in which he disregards Raison's admonition (vv. 69–72), unable to resist the "torrent qui [l']entraîne" (v. 93). Cotin's poetry, however, incites only fear and loathing from his unfortunate audience (vv. 243–46), whereas the speaker's efforts in *Satire VII* provoked pleasure and amusement. Superficial similarity between Cotin and the speaker should not surprise us: *Satire IV* did not exempt the speaker from the reality of universal folly, with the caveat that some are more foolish than others. The speaker in no way negates his thesis that reason is a curse. Completely dissociated from wisdom, it also separates man from nature, yet in itself it is ultimately useless, since man does not obey its dictates. This remains true for the newlywed, the merchant, the glory-hunter, the judge, the scholar—and the poet!

Deserted by all around him whenever his "Démon" (cf. the *manie* of *Satires IV* and *VII*) compels him to declaim his verse, the hapless Cotin represents all mankind. With neither nature's wisdom nor his much vaunted reason to assist him, Everyman Cotin, abandoned by all, stands alone in the world (cf. les "Petites-Maisons" [*IV,* v. 4]). The shift from the exemplum of Cotin to that of the donkey in the concluding section of the poem relies simultaneously on comic association and dialectical principles. The donkey, "instruit par la nature" (v. 247) to obey his instincts, stands in obvious contrast to man (Cotin), whose "bizarre voix" (v. 249) is presumably more dissonant than even the donkey's legendary bray:[46]

> Un Asne pour le moins instruit par la nature,
> A l'instinct qui le guide obeit sans murmure:
> Ne va point follement de sa bizarre voix,
> Défier aux chansons les oiseaux dans les bois.
>
> (vv. 247–50)

Man's super-asinine audacity in challenging the beauty of the birdsongs with his own "chansons" not only reinforces man's denial of nature but also the inanity of such "poets" as Cotin, who insist on reciting their poems to their anguished audience.

The donkey's astute reluctance to set his voice against the birds' melodies—to aspire to be something other than what he is (unlike Cotin)—subtly brings to mind the well-known mythological cautionary tale of King Midas, whose ill-advised aesthetic judgments earned him a pair of donkey's ears.[47] The donkey emerges as a superior judge in the domain of aesthetics.

To recapitulate the eternal inconsistency of reason, the speaker appropriately returns to the image of aimless movement (vv. 35–39, 57–58, 74–76, 94, 236–38), in opposition to the donkey: "Sans avoir la raison il marche sur la route" (v. 251). In vv. 257–58 an enumeration of verbs succinctly summarizing man's hopeless misdirection describes the lover, merchant, miser, and glory-hound who marched in the speaker's introductory parade of fools: "Son esprit au hazard aime, évite, poursuit, / Défait, refait, augmente, oste, éleve, detruit." Man's delusional propensity to worship graven images and his numerous superstitions reverse the Christian doctrine of the divinely created and sanctioned man : animal :: master : subordinate relationship that the speaker challenged in his opening arguments in vv. 1–4. The professor's masterful creature who "Dans le tour d'un compas a mesuré les Cieux" (v. 166) cowers in fear before the number thirteen (v. 261)! Man's ability to forge the very images that he prays to ("Adorer le metal que lui-mesme il fit fondre" [v. 268]) merely confirms this topsy-turvy, insecure irrationality. Also recalling the initial verses of the poem, the geographical sweep of this contradictory behavior (vv. 270–72) provides an ironical contrast with the cramped mental confines that such practices expose.

Man's "upside down" adoration of idols, superstitious fears, and beast worship prompts the speaker to reverse the normal hierarchy by elevating the lowly donkey to the rank of final authority, a fitting mouthpiece for the speaker in the poem's conclusion. The donkey's position as indirect *porte-parole* permits the speaker to sidestep the paradox inherent in any systematic condemnation of human reason: How can the human satirist—richly endowed with the very reason that he so roundly mocks—justify his assault on the very faculty that he himself uses to such devastating effect?[48] How can he claim (implicitly, to be sure) exemption from humanity's imperfections? In *Satire IV* the speaker postulated the existence of varying degrees of *folie*. In this poem the cosmic scale of the speaker's attack precludes such fine distinctions within the human race. Here the answer lies in a "second" speaker whose views are approvingly reported by the main speaker.

In vv. 275–79 the Docteur obligingly provides the speaker the opportunity to confer the power of speech on his donkey/sage.[49] Thus the donkey—according to the Docteur, "le joüet de tous les animaux, / Un stupide Animal, sujet à mille maux" (vv. 277–78)—is cast in the role of adjudicator in the debate. That he is "sujet à mille maux" incriminates man's cruel treatment of the long-suffering, stolid jackass.[50] The traditional butt of ridicule becomes the definitive expert whose "last word" will determine how we are to ponder the problem of man and reason. Divine wisdom naturally sides with the virtuous donkey/speaker, whose intent is not merely to taunt humankind, but to assist Heaven in humanity's reformation (vv. 283–84). In this vein, the elevation of the donkey brings to mind Christ's words on eternal life, "But many that are first shall be last; and the last shall be first" (Matt. 19.30).

Not unlike the speaker in Juvenal's *Satire I,* who directs his invective at the passers-by in a Roman street scene, the donkey "promene sa veuë" (v. 288) on a busy Parisian thoroughfare. Intensifying the "biological" focus of the poem announced in vv. 1–4, the zoologist-donkey's empirical observations dehumanize the objects of his examination. The genus collectively called "Hommes" (v. 289) exhibits a diversity of colors displayed according to its function in its "natural" habitat. Color displays accompany additional specialized adaptations that distinguish various species, for example, the physician, "un Assassin en housse" (v. 292), from "un escadron fouré" (v. 293) of professors. The parade of pedants mirrors the "grosse compagnie" that leads another species of the genus "Hommes" to a most unnatural death (vv. 295–96). Incredibly, such aberrant behavior is sanctioned by a swarm of subspecies (belonging to the species designated "Justice" [v. 295]), "les Juges, les Huissiers, / Les Clercs, les Procureurs, les Sergens, les Greffiers" (vv. 301–02), whose combined auditory signals seem to come from that most unnatural of locales, hell itself:

> Ou qu'il voit la Justice en grosse compagnie,
> Mener tuer un homme avec ceremonie?
> Que pense-t-il de nous? lors que sur le midi
> Un hazard au Palais le conduit un Jeudi;
> Lors qu'il entend de loin, d'une gueule infernale,
> La Chicane en fureur mugir dans la grand'Sale?
> (vv. 295–300)

Man's reason has contrived to establish a system of regulations that legitimize killing his own kind. Boileau's almost Voltairean verses effectively register his own shock and the horror that such brutish behavior should provoke in us.

In the poem's final line ("Ma foi, non plus que nous; l'Homme n'est qu'une beste!" [v. 308]), the scientific donkey pronounces in a human voice a judgment based on his observations. His use of inductive reasoning aside, the donkey ("Sans avoir la raison . . ." [v. 251]) reduces man to the level of beast. The obvious pun on the last word, *beste,* permits his conclusion to play on two levels. On the zoological plane, the scientist/donkey perceives, "De tous costez" (v. 305), that at best man exhibits behavior similar to that of the other members of the animal kingdom. On a moral plane, however, the satirist/donkey castigates humanity's innate stupidity and unique brutality. The alternating rhythms of expansion and contraction so basic to the poem's thematic structure coexist in the authoritative jackass's verdict. The mystery of man's place in the cosmos, a perplexing metaphysical question vast in scope, is in effect resolved in a sweeping *reductio ad bestiam.* Armed with his newly found, eloquent voice, the speechless jackass overcomes his customary inarticulate brays, thus anticipating the principal theme of the ensuing *Satire IX.* Prominent in *Satire VII* and seemingly settled in *VIII,* the struggle between protest and silence will linger on.

Chapter Six

Withdrawal

The playful tone of the speaker/donkey's reductive pronouncement at the close of *Satire VIII* brusquely shifts in the following poem. Like *Satire VII,* an internal debate between two elemental voices in the speaker's aesthetic psyche, *Satire IX* is reiterative, operating as a comprehensive conclusion to the preceding nine poems.[1] Implicit and explicit systematic allusions to images and themes of the *Discours au Roy* and *Satires I* to *VIII* amplify the resumptive function of *Satire IX.*

In its contemptuous and angry reproof to "mon Esprit," the first voice immediately recalls the words and character of Raison as portrayed in *Satire VII,* vv. 69–73, where a reproachful "on" advised "Pauvre Esprit" to desist from the perilous genre of satire.[2] The speaker's insistence on his own pleasure and instinctive inclination for this "méchant métier" (*VII,* v. 2) in turn provoked his attitude toward Raison in *Satire IV:*

> Souvent de nos maux la Raison est le pire.
> C'est Elle qui farouche, au milieu des plaisirs,
> D'un remords importun vient brider nos desirs.
> La Fâcheuse a pour nous des rigueurs sans pareilles;
> C'est un Pêdant qu'on a sans cesse à ses oreilles.
>
> (vv. 114–18)

The stiffly formal, condescending demeanor and sharp, self-righteous tone of the first voice in *Satire IX* conjures up this *trouble-fête* "Fâcheuse." Forbearance at long last exhausted, the voice I shall call Raison has yet again launched into a long lecture, in effect sternly interrupting the burlesque hijinks of Esprit's talking jackass in *Satire VIII:*[3] "Mais puisque vous poussez ma patience à bout, / Une fois en ma vie, il faut vous dire tout" (vv. 5–6).

Explicit reference in v. 10 to the interlocutor of *Satire VIII* assures continuity between the two poems. Esprit's freewheeling assault on Raison in the preceding poem at length prompts this explosion of anger and frustration. Raison minces no words in his harsh attack on Esprit's moral sense and lack of self-control. Esprit's audacious pronouncements in *Satire VIII* on man's place in the cosmos here receive ironic commentary in vv. 11–12: "Qu'estant seul à couvert des traits de la Satire, / Vous avez tout pouvoir de parler et d'écrire." In *Satire IX* Raison intends to turn the tables. In his blunt judgment, Esprit's numerous "défauts" (v. 2), his "jeux criminels" and "insolence" (v. 4), are an elaborate disguise concealing an absence of real poetic taste and inspiration. Tautologically labeling the *Satires* "libres caprices" (v. 7), Raison condemns the sense of anarchic liberation that the *Satires* might provide the reader. Raison's frank amusement at Esprit's serious wish to "reformer la ville" (v. 16) underscores the profound rift between these two components of the speaker's mind.

Conversely, Raison reveals character traits that connect him to the free-spirited, impudent Esprit. In the midst of his nagging and patronizing reprimands, Raison lets fly brief satirical barbs that are strangely reminiscent of Esprit's distinctive manner. In v. 18 a humorous aside mocks the lawyer Gautier's caustic intensity. In vv. 27–28 the aspersion cast on l'Abbé de Pure harks back to the first derisive slur of *Satire II:* "Si je veux d'un Galant dépeindre la figure, / Ma plume pour rimer trouve l'Abbé de Pure" (vv. 17–18). These reflexlike movements of that "quinteuse" (*II,* v. 16), *la Rime,* in *Satire IX* expose a kind of central nervous system that ties together Esprit and Raison, which are, after all, linked components of our speaker's mind.[4] Suggested by the unrelenting questions posed by Raison in vv. 19–28, a third, unnamed, figure linking the two figures enters the picture and provides the answer to Raison's queries (". . . Quelle verve indiscrette / Sans l'aveu des neuf Sœurs, vous a rendu Poëte?" [vv. 19–20]). *Satire VII* assists the reader: it is, of course, the ever-present Muse who controls Esprit. Not surprisingly, the down-to-earth, "sensible" voice of Raison is totally oblivious to the Muse's commands.[5] We must not forget that the Muse is an "esprit divin" (v. 22)!

Insulting his Muse as an agent of an evil destiny, "Cet ascendant malin qui vous force à rimer" (v. 30), Raison suggests—

following the example of *Satire VII*—the alternative genre of *panégyrique.* Allusions to the *Discours au Roy* and *Satire I* aside,[6] Raison's view of poetry as a commodity to be bought and sold and his expectation that "l'espoir du gain" (v. 35) would invigorate the Muse confirm his blindness to the intimate relationship between Esprit and Muse, as we saw in *Satire VII.* Not surprisingly, the "lightweight" verse ("une once de fumée" [v. 36]) that Esprit might concoct would paradoxically become a ponderous burden, ultimately suppressing the free flow of satirical inspiration bestowed by the Muse (cf. *Discours au Roy,* vv. 9–10; *VII,* vv. 43, 93).

Esprit's response is familiar. Each "Chantre" (v. 39) must adhere to his own manner; the only acceptable alternative is silence. From this, the reader would anticipate that the speaker's satirical mode might materialize—instinctively—whenever he gives voice to his thoughts. His reply to a disdainful Raison on the possibility of writing the poetry of accolade in vv. 37–51, however, ironically incorporates accolade as well as the usual barbs. A parody of circumstantial poetry's pompous style ("sur le ton d'un Orphée") in vv. 40–42[7] and, conversely, the respect accorded Racan as a panegyrist admirably adept in his genre (vv. 43–44) provide models that poets like himself and Cotin, who share "l'amour de blâmer" (v. 46), must avoid:

> Mais pour Cotin et moi, qui rimons au hazard:
> Que l'amour de blâmer fit Poëtes par art,
> Quoi qu'un tas de Grimauds vante nostre éloquence,
> Le plus seur est pour nous de garder le silence.
>
> (vv. 45–48)

Like the praise given the estimable Racan, the association with Boileau's nemesis Cotin is unexpected. Having dabbled in both satire, for which he apparently has "amour" (v. 46),[8] and in panegyric, Cotin is the prime example of a poet who has followed his own Raison's advice. As tokens of an undiscerning audience, the "tas de Grimauds" in v. 47, i.e., ignorant schoolboys or pedantic windbags, who swoon over commonplace "éloquence" recall the "moindres Grimauds" in *Satire IV* (v. 92) who knew enough to spurn Chapelain's rhymes. Indeed, the reference to a witless readership suggests a major theme of *Satire II* (where Georges de Scudéry's books inevitably find "Un Marchand pour les vendre, et des Sots pour les lire" [*II,* v. 82]) as well as the faceless mass of tasteless dinner guests in *Satire III.*

Esprit's modest avowal of "foiblesse" (v. 51) as a justification for his rejection of elegy prompts a typically judgmental reaction from Raison in vv. 52–60. Moral "mollesse,"[9] not inaptitude, explains the unprovoked, "irrational" assaults that the speaker's black bile spews forth. Blunt accusations of pure malevolence and even irreligion accompany the usual warnings about the dangers, physical and financial, that such work presents to the unthinking poet (cf. *VII,* vv. 69–72).

But admonishment as to present perils shifts to arguments based on that preoccupation of all poets, one's place in the vast temporal continuum encompassing literary ancestors and descendants. Beginning at v. 61, Raison's case can be interpreted as a direct response to Esprit's assurance in *Satire VII* that he is following in the path of the great Roman satirists Lucilius, Horace, and Juvenal (*VII,* vv. 73–80). While enlarging the terms of the debate, Raison's acid reminder ("Et déjà vous croyez dans vos rimes obscures, / Aux Saumaizes futurs préparer des tortures" [vv. 63–64]) that only a happy few poets will ever find enduring admiration also belittles lowly, ephemeral satire as the genre *least* likely to win lasting fame. The allusion to the myth of Icarus in vv. 55–56 epitomizes Raison's poetic perspective: Esprit must endeavor to "fly," to create lofty works even at the risk of singed wings, to reach for heaven itself (cf. *Discours au Roy,* vv. 13–14). Earth- and time-bound, the satirical Esprit occupies the nethermost regions of the poetic landscape, not unlike the contemptible Abbé de Pure, who "rampe dans la fange" (v. 28) while a Horace or a Voiture soars to the summit of Parnassus.[10]

Another series of queries begins at v. 83, prefaced by Raison's contention that even if Esprit's hope for immortality comes to pass, constant harassment in one's lifetime from a legion of victims cannot compensate for the uncertain satisfaction of future renown. Paradoxically, the successful satirist's legacy ("Faire sifler Cotin chez nos derniers neveux" [v. 82]) rests on man's petty spite and malice and relies on the pathetic Cotins of the world. In v. 82 the burlesque mingling of high and low styles underlines the disparity between the noble poet's appeal to the lofty in man's nature and the satirist's dependence on bad poets and low style to make his reputation. Raison's questions concerning present financial hardship, and a fearful and hostile readership in vv. 83–86, lead inevitably to repeated emphasis on Raison's misconception of Esprit's character and his deep motivation for badmouthing second-rate writers. As in v. 30, a repetitious Raison blames a mysterious agent of evil that compels the satirist: "Quel Démon vous irrite et vous porte à médire?" (v. 87). As before, unbeknownst to Raison, the answer is clear: Esprit's forceful Muse, his "manie" as portrayed especially in *Satires IV* and *VII,* regulates his writing. Armed with ignorance, Raison pursues his argument: Esprit's incessant badgering of literally and figuratively dead poets can only result in the absurd task of resurrecting that which was never endowed with life! Although the real Jonah, David, and Moses may have indeed drawn breath in their long-ago biblical incarnations, contemporary poetic reworkings of these characters have failed miserably to revive these dead heroes (vv. 91-93: ". . . Ceux qui sont morts sont morts" [v. 94]). Since the King himself has not declared such works a criminal offense, why should the presumptuous satirist torment the authors who produce them? Paris will forever overflow with bad writers, wasting paper and ink, all clamoring to make a name for themselves (vv. 105–12). An aesthetic libertarian, Raison believes that the enterprise of Art can never be controlled.

Despite Raison's rebuke, he obviously believes that wretched writers not only exist, but, more importantly, proliferate in Paris. His technique of enumerating particular examples in vv. 97–98 duplicates a similar device in *Satire VII,* vv. 44–45. That the speakers are ostensibly different in each case—Esprit in one and Raison in the other—again suggests a veiled rapport between the two figures. Despite the dialogue form of the poem, the "separate" voices share a common sensibility that is deeper than the differences enunciated in this debate. On the reality of an eternal plague of bad writers there can be no disagreement. How to react to this blight is another matter altogether, and remains the crux of the argument between the antagonists. Raison's laissez-faire approach contrasts markedly with Esprit's hands-on policy.

Raison's conviction that reform is preposterous is a logical consequence of the pragmatic view that problems should be confronted only when there is a reasonable chance of resolving them. His reliance on the concept of laws, regulations, and customs (vv. 103, 107, 114) as a means of governing Apollo's dominion, and his charge that Esprit's ambition is to institute a "legal code" sanctioning poetic activity, again reveal his fundamental misunderstanding of Esprit. On this matter *Satires IV* and *VII* again assist the reader: Esprit's motivations are founded not so much on the serious notion of *instruire,* but rather on the more agreeable concept of *plaire.* More precisely, he derives personal pleasure in skewering fools:

> Enfin c'est mon plaisir, je veux me satisfaire.
> Je ne puis bien parler, et ne sçaurois me taire;
> Et dès qu'un mot plaisant vient luire à mon esprit,
> Je n'ai point de repos qu'il ne soit en écrit.
>
> (*VII,* vv. 89–92)

In vv. 119–36 Raison's equally misdirected attempt to imagine for the benefit of Esprit the reactions of an antagonistic reader reiterates Raison's own criticisms while simultaneously alluding to prior *Satires.* Esprit's relative youth ("un jeune Fou" [v. 121]) is suggested particularly in *Satire II,* in which the speaker/disciple aspires to emulate the creative genius of Molière. Besides containing an identical hemistich (". . . qui se croit tout permis" [v. 121; *VII,* v. 15]), *Satire VII* focuses on the impulsive, involuntary nature of the speaker's critical assaults ("Et qui pour un bon mot va perdre vingt Amis" [v. 122]) and aims a barb at Chapelain's *Pucelle* (v. 123; *VII,* v. 30). Animosity toward "le Barreau" (v. 125) is especially evident in *Satires I* (vv. 113–28) and *VIII* (vv. 155–60, 295–302). Reference to poverty (". . . un gueux revêtu des dépouilles d'Horace" [v. 128]) evokes *Satire I*'s indigent Damon ("Mais qui n'était vêtu que de simple bureau" [v. 3]), just as mention of the sleep-inducing preacher (v. 126) echoes vv. 147–48: ". . . comme un Docteur, / Allez de vos sermons endormir l'Auditeur." Verse 130 ("Avant lui Juvenal avoit dit en Latin / *Qu'on est assis à l'aise aux sermons de Cotin*" [vv. 129–30]) quotes inaccurately from *Satire III,* vv. 57–60:

> Jugez en cet estat, si je pouvois me plaire,
> Moy qui ne conte rien ni le vin, ni la chere;

> Si l'on n'est plus au large assis en un festin,
> Qu'aux sermons de Cassaigne, ou de l'Abbé Cotin.

In vv. 131–33 persistent accusations of Boileau's plagiarism ("Il cherche à se couvrir de ces noms glorieux" [v. 133]) allude to *Satires II* ("Sur la rime") and *VII,* where Esprit defends his vocation by direct reference to the noble example of his Latin predecessors:

> Hé quoi? lors qu'autrefois Horace après Lucile,
> Exhaloit en bons mots les vapeurs de sa bile,
> Et vangeant la vertu par des traits éclatans,
> Alloit oster le masque aux vices de son temps:
> Ou bien quand Juvenal de sa mordante plume,
> Faisant couler des flots de fiel et d'amertume,
> Gourmandoit en couroux tout le peuple Latin,
> L'un ou l'autre fit-il une tragique fin?
>
> (*VII,* vv. 73–80)

Finally, vv. 135–36 reflect the *Discours au Roy,* vv. 138–40, wherein the speaker comically abandons the ship of panegyric as he recognizes that he is ill-adapted to the genre. This "typical" reader's disparagement at least demonstrates that Esprit's poetic efforts have found an attentive, if not accommodating, audience.

The question of audience reaction continues: Raison attributes this enmity to the fear that the satirist's ridicule provokes among his readers. Although unnamed, the sensitive reader may imagine faults within himself similar to those targeted by Esprit: "Rien n'appaise un Lecteur toûjours tremblant d'effroi, / Qui voit peindre en autrui ce qu'il remarque en soi" (vv. 141–42). *Satire VII* has already covered this ground: "Un discours trop sincère aisément nous outrage. / Chacun dans ce miroir pense voir son visage" (vv. 17–18). Although Raison admonishes Esprit, he cannot deny that Esprit's sincere outbursts of rancor incite equally genuine reactions in its readers, that good satire by its very nature strives for this effect. It is far different indeed from ". . . un froid panegyrique, / [qui] Peut pourir à son aise au fond d'une boutique" (*VII,* vv. 9–10). Satire's air of impulsive vitality plays a large part in Esprit's addiction to the genre. What Raison calls "fureurs" (v. 146), suggesting irrationality, Esprit might label intense enthusiasm for the excitement of the arena and the fray ("affaires nouvelles" / "querelles" [vv. 143–44]).

Esprit's reply makes a crucial distinction between "droite Raison," who speaks in vv. 153–56, and the allegorical attributes of his interlocutor, the character I call Raison. This "droite Raison" has more to do with the notion of *bon sens,* which Brody defines as "an abstract literary quality or creative faculty that confers splendor and value on the whole poem as well as its parts."[11] This of course is far removed from that other Raison:

> C'est un Pêdant qu'on a sans cesse à ses oreilles,
> Qui toûjours nous gourmande, et loin de nous toucher,
> Souvent, comme Joli, perd son temps à prescher.
> (*IV,* vv. 118–20)

The "impertinent Auteur" (v. 153) who demolishes right reason on every page elicits an instinctive response from an incensed Esprit. This impulsive reaction corresponds to the barking dog analogy prominent in *Satire VII,* vv. 56–58:

> Mais tout Fat me déplaist et me blesse les yeux.
> Je le poursuis par tout, comme un chien fait sa proye,
> Et ne le sens jamais, qu'aussi-tost je n'aboye.

Besides reviving the image of weightlessness and emptiness in v. 36, v. 156 exploits nasal assonance ("*Et ces riens enfermez dans de grandes paroles?*") to evoke *Satire VII*'s snarling dog that instantly—and instinctively—turns on the source of its anger. This spontaneous, thus sincere, reaction to insults to right reason must be distinguished from simple *médisance,* a charge habitually directed toward the satirist Esprit (e.g., vv. 52–54; *VII,* vv. 2, 7). Yet another speaker, a "Fourbe," provides an illustration in vv. 161–64 of witty, premeditated badmouthing that Esprit equates with pure malice. Esprit asserts that this example of two-faced "adresse" (v. 165) is quite different from the protest of natural instincts that are compelled to revolt whenever dullness ("un Fat" [v. 151]) offends *la droite Raison.* Fortunately, he is "Un Esprit né sans fard, sans basse complaisance" (v. 167), which also explains his native incapacity for panegyric.

Esprit affirms his fundamental rights as a reader to evaluate literary productions and to make his judgments known. Even in the hierarchized society in which he moves, every individual possesses this prerogative: "un Sot de qualité" (v. 173); "Un Clerc" (v. 177); "Valet d'Auteur," "Copiste" (v. 181). The reader's Bill of Rights does not of course guarantee that the individual's opinion will conform to right reason's dictates. The system of "justice"[12] by which a writer's fate is determined may be, however, just as ineffective as the real legal system that tries genuine crimes and that Esprit has already attacked in previous poems. For this reason Esprit feels particularly the obligation to speak out against ridiculous writers as well as their equally misguided readers.

As in other sections of the poem, prior *Satires* resurface in vv. 165–90. The ignoble noble ("un Sot de qualité" [v. 173]) exemplifies the "vaine noblesse" (v. 6) of *Satire V* whose "lâche et molle oisiveté" (*V,* v. 20) negates his illustrious name. His erroneous views concerning various poets, juxtaposed with the law clerk's attitude toward Corneille in vv. 177–80, echo *Satire III,* vv. 170–200, in which the drunken dinner guests pronounce equally perverse verdicts. Finally, the speaker's comments regarding the author-reader dichotomy and the relative qualities of each bring to mind *Satire II*'s attack on dreadful poets who nonetheless acquire "Un Marchand pour les vendre, et des Sots pour les lire" (v. 82).

Allied to the poet-audience relationship, the question of the writer's present and future reputation undergoes further development beginning at v. 191. This issue, of course, lies at the heart of the dispute between Esprit's quest for unfettered self-expression and Raison's desire for self-censorship. Esprit's disingenuous questions in vv. 191–98 as to the source of his victims' outrage allows him comically to reveal their deep-seated motivations. Esprit's practice of *naming* the butt of his ridicule—conspicuously remarked upon in v. 203 by a disapproving reader—exposes his enemies' fear that his appraisals will long outlast the current generation. His contention that the Cotins of Paris and their like owe their present and future fame to him alone, and that the genre of satire willingly provides this immortality service, is an effective—and funny—way of further degrading his adversaries while justifying his own poetic enterprise and the implied eternal renown that he himself will enjoy!

After a corroboration of Esprit's perception that most readers agree with him yet lack the courage to say so (vv. 201–02), another negative voice speaks out in vv. 203–07. An innovation in contemporary satire, Boileau's bold naming of his victims prompts this naive reader reaction ("*Attaquer Chapelain! ah! c'est un si bon Homme*" [v. 204]). Identification of author with man blandly ignores the conventions of literary procedure that form the basis of the satirist's art. Just as the persona cannot be taken as the pure voice of the actual writer, the names of those whom the speaker attacks go well beyond the living, or dead, persons who carry these names. Once again Esprit pleads innocent to the charge of malicious intent. Chapelain may indeed be an exemplary human being, yet once he establishes himself as a writer his literary persona is created through the audience reception process: "Dès que l'impression fait éclore un Poëte, / Il est esclave né de quiconque l'achète" (vv. 183–84). At this point, his name betokens a kind of allegorical figure who may represent positive or negative literary currents: it has absolutely nothing to do with the character of the flesh and blood human being behind it.

The key to understanding Esprit in vv. 208–24 centers on his attitude toward the author (one called "Chapelain" in this case) as *example* for others who may or may not appreciate his qualities and/or defects. Recalling the thematics of *Satires II* and *V* with their emphasis on Molière and Louis XIV, respectively, as ideal models, the speaker stresses his belief in the pivotal importance of example in life and in art:

> Mais que pour un modele, on montre ses écrits,
> Qu'il soit le mieux renté de tous les beaux Esprits:
> Comme Roi des Auteurs, qu'on l'éleve à l'Empire:
> Ma bile alors s'échauffe, et je brûle d'écrire.
>
> (vv. 217–20)

Satire VIII's juxtaposition of Cotin and the jackass, with its implicit allusion to King Midas's donkey ears, anticipated specific reference to the Midas story in vv. 222–24.[13] This parable clarifies Esprit's next point, reinforced with the famous example of *Le Cid* ("Tout Paris pour Chimene a les yeux de Rodrigue" [v. 232]), that, fortunately for art, works of genius will triumph over all obstacles and that the inferior writer's donkey ears can never be long hidden. Despite this optimistic view, the Midas parable insists on the power of "ce Barbier" (v. 222), who, like the satirist, had the courage to divulge the naked, distasteful truth that the "typical" reader in vv. 203–07 cannot bring himself to express. In this perspective, the speaker/satirist becomes the ideal—model—reader who cuts through the sundry personal discomforts and complications that arise whenever forthright opinion collides with private sensibilities.

Esprit begins his peroration at v. 243 by summarizing the now familiar objections to satire raised in this poem as well as others. These are:

1. its restricted audience. This obtains not only in the present but in the future as well.

2. its dangers. Here the example of Régnier reinforces the argument.[14]

3. its deceptive charms. Making a laughingstock of others is a selfish, even un-Christian, pleasure.

4. its aesthetic superiority to other genres. The ever popular panegyric comes to mind!

5. its moral nullity. Satire does not edify; it cannot reform man.

Again declaring his ineptitude in other genres, Esprit expands on his opening defensive gambit in vv. 38–42. Since the satiric persona must differ in character, emotion, means, intent, and circumstances from the *je* of a Malherbian ode, for example, another speaker, set off by italics, articulates the grandiose Malherbian manner in vv. 252–56. That the satiric *je* would attempt an ode would be just as "mal à propos" (v. 256) as an equally inappropriate stab at pastoral poetry, where the urban satirist, completely *dépaysé,* would be particularly ridiculous. Like the eclogue, Esprit views *galant* poetry as artificial, insincere, and even decadent. Obviously, the candidly blunt, irreverent, ironical *je* of satire could never seriously perform his generic role in circumstantial, pastoral, or *amoureux* poetry. Again echoing *Satire V*'s contempt for the *mollesse* (v. 266) of the false, decadent aristocrat (*V,* vv. 5, 20, 136), Esprit opts for the unadorned honesty and moral strength of the truly noble character.

After defending his own moral integrity in vv. 243–66, Esprit champions the genre to which he owes allegiance. The essentially virtuous stance of the genre rests upon assets familiar to the classicist: its skillful commingling of "le plaisant et l'utile" (v. 268), its potential for innovation, its capacity for correcting humanity's moral flaws, its boldness, and its power over "l'orgueil et l'injustice" (v. 271). Satire's status as the bastion of right reason also rests firmly upon its illustrious history. As in *Satire VII* (". . . Horace après Lucile, / Exhaloit en bons mots les vapeurs de sa bile" [vv. 73–74]), the speaker exploits the multiple meanings of the expression "bon mot" in v. 273 to underline the wit as well as the moralizing value of satire past and present:

> C'est ainsi que Lucile appuyé de Lélie,
> Fit justice en son temps des Cotins d'Italie,
> Et qu'Horace jettant le sel à pleines mains,
> Se joüoit aux dépens des Pelletiers Romains.
> (vv. 275–78)

The speaker again (cf. *VII,* vv. 73–80) suggests clear analogies between himself and past masters Lucilius[15] and Horace. That the latter threw handfuls of salt—an ancient metaphor for biting wit—reinforces the concept of literary generations inasmuch as Horace used the same metaphor for *his* artistic forefather Lucilius in *Satires* I.10.3–4: "at idem, quod sale multo / urbem defricuit, charta laudatur eadem."[16] The generic Roman "Cotins" and "Pelletiers" who once provided rich satiric fodder for Lucilius and Horace were to Rome in their respective lifetimes as Esprit's victims are to present-day Paris. As in many prior *Satires,* the metonymies suggest a faceless multitude of ubiquitous poetasters whose numbers match their timelessness.[17]

Even from his impressionable youth ("C'est Elle qui m'ouvrant le chemin qu'il faut suivre, / M'inspira dés quinze ans la haine d'un sot livre" [vv. 279–80]), Esprit's hatred for literary dullness was nurtured by his artistic ancestors Lucilius and Horace. Esprit was welcomed into the loving family called Satire, which taught him to walk (v. 282). Satire "raised" him. Repudiating this bloodline would be akin to the contemptible behavior of the false noble in *Satire V,* who betrays the lustrous example of his forebears. His personal honor hangs in the balance, for, like a true knight, he has sworn to consecrate his artistic life to Satire.

As the notable member of this venerable clan of Satire that he proudly proclaims himself to be, Esprit mockingly feigns meek submission to Raison's demands and, quite in character, sarcastically repudiates his former views in vv. 284–94. His mock-serious atonement in vv. 284–86 mediates between the earnest declaration of fealty of vv. 267–83 and the burlesque declaration of renunciation in vv. 288–94. As before, prior *Satires* are inevitably conjured up as he pronounces his *mea culpa.*[18] Esprit's craven "rejection" of his formerly unshakable views is so sarcastically stated as to be unmistakable, especially in view of *Satire VII,* in which the speaker patiently and unequivocally confessed his inability to "changer de stile" (*IX,* v. 287). Yet literal-minded, tedious Raison, also in character, approves of Esprit's counterfeit change of heart ("—Bon, mon Esprit, courage, poursuivez" [v. 294]), proving, not surprisingly, that he is incapable of recognizing the most obvious literary strategies. This "model" reader/listener, devoid of taste and possessed of zero critical acumen, is of the same stripe as the numerous incompetent audiences so decried in prior poems, most notably *Satires I, II,* and *III.*

Despite the farcical incomprehension of Raison, his reaction raises a crucial problem inherent in satire and which the speaker in the *Discours au Roy* treated at length. The inveterate satirist will find it practically impossible to make any sincere statement—especially one in praise of an idea or individual—that cannot be taken as ironic ridicule by his readers, be they of good will or ill will. Besides underlining his dull single-mindedness, Raison's comic warnings about ill-willed readers ("Mais ne voyez-vous pas que leur Troupe en furie, / Va prendre encor ces vers pour une raillerie?" [vv. 295–96]) who will choose to misinterpret Esprit's "repentance" provide substantial proof of the profound *mésalliance* and thus the disagreement between the reality and the pleasure principles within the speaker's psyche. Whatever his defective personal reading of Esprit's words, Raison's admonishment reveals on the other hand his understanding of the "Troupe en furie" (v. 295) of "Rimeurs blessez" (v. 298) who will rise up to muzzle the voice that dares to mock them. That Raison can possess and impart knowledge based on past, empirically demonstrable behavior and accordingly predict future conduct, yet be so aesthetically obtuse, points up acute intellectual limitations that Esprit apparently does not share.

In spite of Raison's aesthetic deficiencies and the resulting misunderstandings, he remains, above all, sympathetic to Esprit and distressed over what he perceives as Esprit's reckless denial of indisputable truths. Once again depicted as a faceless mob of malevolent charlatans, his enemies will, Raison fears, eventually embroil the naive Esprit in political intrigues that will bring upon him the wrath of the King himself. Raison's conventional belief that royal panegyrics are the poet's best defense against such calumny returns us to the subjects of patronage, loyalty, honor, and the contemporary poet's societal obligations and accountability that were especially prominent both in the collections's introductory poem, the *Discours au Roy,* and the median poem within the *Satires* proper, *Satire V,* "Sur la Noblesse." This return to origins re-emphasizes the King's status as antithesis to the countless, mendacious "Sots" (v. 317) who solicit his largesse. Esprit's reverence for the King expressed here and most notably in the prior two poems supports his contention that Louis XIV can distinguish false from true value.[19] Besides reiterating a major element of the *Discours au Roy,* his professed indifference to pecuniary advantage (vv. 312–14) puts him on the same level as *Satire V*'s true nobleman, whose worth derives uniquely from intrinsic moral qualities, and not from glittering facade.

Raison's tone shift in the course of the poem from exasperated censor to caring, even loving, ally betrays the intimate emotional rapport between these dissimilar entities within the speaker's psyche. In v. 319 three words—"Je vous crois"—summarize the essential bond of trust between Esprit and Raison. Moreover, the latter's confidence in his soul mate tends to enhance the rhetorical force of Esprit's protestation of sincerity in his admiration of Louis XIV. Despite Raison's faith in his integrity and Esprit's assurances of future prudence ("On me verra toûjours sage dans mes caprices" [v. 315]), Raison clings doggedly to the fear that a well-placed "Auteur en couroux" will bring down insouciant, irresponsible Esprit. An echo of Raison in the poem's opening (cf. v. 7), his use of the word *caprices* shows his underlying sympathy for Raison, yet may also be an ironical commentary on Raison's earlier use of the word. Indeed, if we wish to question, disingenuously, every apparently sincere position set forth by Esprit, his declaration of admiration for the King may be considered to be of the same cloth as his "conversion" in vv. 288–94. Although the average sensitive reader should be capable of discerning the differing modes of style (". . . je vais changer de stile" [v. 287]) manipulated in these two accolades, ambiguity necessarily exists, permitting the ill-willed or obtuse reader (for example, the countless "Cotins" and "Pelletiers" [vv. 276 and 278]) to misread the playful satirist to suit his own, selfish, purposes.

In this light, Raison's last words provide the only absolutely foolproof solution to the satirist's predicament. In the face of a vicious audience who may already possess, or will endeavor to find, the means to destroy Esprit, Raison insists that discreet self-censorship must overrule impetuous bravado. Like *Satire IV,* the poem's conclusion, while furnishing highly effective developmental closure, sounds an ambivalent—and quite unexpected—note. This ambivalence rests upon the clash between Esprit's unrelenting self-assurance, superior wits, and seeming determination to pursue his Muse, and the poem's "last word" resolution. Boileau in fact did not publish another poem labeled "Satire" for twenty-six years after *Satire IX* first appeared in 1668.[20] Accordingly, it can rightly be said that Esprit actually acquiesced in Raison's firm "Taisez-vous," although Boileau's Muse obviously practiced various other genres during this long "silence."[21]

Contemplated in *Satire VII,* Esprit's burlesque change of *stile* in v. 287 ("Puis que vous le voulez, je vais changer de stile") thus becomes a reality after *Satire IX.* Boileau's turn to other genres marks an important point in his artistic career, indicating a developing attitude toward the function of poetry, and, perhaps, pointing to a change in the social status of Boileau himself.[22] Whatever the explanation, in poetic terms Raison, despite his donkey's ear level of aesthetic appreciation, succeeded in suppressing insouciant, subversive Esprit.[23] The vigorous pleasure principle that we hear in the droll voice of Esprit in *Satire IX* will yield to another, more sober speaker in the later poems.

Satire IX thus ends on a note of withdrawal. The main theme of the first *Satire* recounting the failed poet's bitter departure from Paris comes full circle, to focus on another kind of retreat, less acrimonious, but equally definitive. Esprit's firmly stated commitment to celebrate the King's glory on the basis of his own certainty that Louis XIV justly deserves such praise, and not merely as a means to reap material rewards, returns the reader to the fundamental theme of the *Discours au Roy.* Above all else, Louis XIV's divinely inspired judgment can distinguish honesty from duplicity. *Epistre I* explicitly reiterates the intent to withdraw from "satire," associated at the end of *Satire IX* with professional, social, and physical dangers, to pursue a nobler goal:

> Pour moi, qui sur Ton nom déja brûlant d'écrire
> Sens au bout de ma plume expirer la Satire,
> Je n'ose de mes vers vanter ici le prix.
> Toutefois, si quelqu'un de mes foibles écrits
> Des ans injurieux peut éviter l'outrage,
> Peut-estre pour Ta gloire aura-t-il son usage.
> (*Epistre I,* vv. 177–81)

Hence, the impetuous Esprit will retreat from the fray, not of course to seek refuge in "quelque antre ou quelque roche" (*Satire I,* v. 25) as did Damon, but to find another "stile," another bearing, in an evolving poetic career.[24]

Conclusion

The overriding presence and personality of the speaker dominate the early *Satires*. At every bend in this multifaceted construct the reader encounters this creative figure, underpinning and thus reinforcing the intertextual connections predicated on theme, image, causality, logic, tonality, syntax, and association. The preceding analyses have attempted to demonstrate the importance of his determining voice in the poems. The character whom we call the speaker or the poet's persona emerges as a vibrant human being, full of self-doubt and contradictions, equally as complex as the contemporaneous Arnolphe or Andromaque.

In formal verse satire it has long been accepted as axiomatic that the speaker exhibits character traits that are inherent in the poet's own psychological makeup. While we must not betray the literariness of the *Satires* by looking upon them as an autobiographical exercise, it is nonetheless essential for the informed reader to assume that the character of the speaker in these poems originates in and thus derives from the poet himself. For this reason Borgerhoff in his groundbreaking work on Boileau spoke of the lyricism in this apparently rigid classical writer. Borgerhoff attempts to delimit the myriad guises of Boileau—literary critic, social commentator, satirist, poet, careerist, etc.—and to focus on

> the obvious fact that very much of his verse is implicitly or explicitly about *him*self. . . . Satire was, I suppose, Boileau's way, as the fable was La Fontaine's way, of beating the game and of expressing *himself* with freedom in an age which had done so much to discourage lyricism.[1]

The peculiar situation of the satirist/speaker establishes a special relationship between himself and his audience. Obliged to satisfy his readers that his vituperations are well-founded, and not the products of personal vindictiveness or rank prejudice, the satirical speaker must maintain at least a semblance of upright virtue.[2] His objective, after all, is to censure dullness whenever and wherever he may find it. The speaker thus maintains a balancing act, since the guise of *vir bonus,* however necessary, must not drift into unctuous rectitude or piety, which would repel the model *honnête homme* reader.[3] To facilitate the reader's understanding of the speaker, his public stance and, more importantly, his private side combine to create a finely nuanced persona. The result is a person with whom the reader may feel marked empathy. On one level then, verse satire as Boileau practiced it might be viewed more as a study in character than a playful but serious commentary on society's foibles.

Contrary to the staid classical image that has persisted since the publication of *L'Art poétique* in 1674, Boileau's persona in the early *Satires* has traits in common with the standard *libertin* ideology of the early part of the century, traditionally associated with the figure of Théophile de Viau as examined by such scholars as Antoine Adam and René Pintard.[4] While hardly revolutionary, *Satire VIII*'s insistence on the primacy of nature over reason as the criterion of universal truth questions orthodox philosophy's first principles. In this and other *Satires* Boileau's neglect of God, the soul, and the essentiality of reason as officially promulgated by the Church and State stems from the satirist's perception of the disparity between abstract conceptions and the reality that he observes everywhere around him, exaggerated, of course, for comic effect. The spiritual vocabulary used to elucidate Damon's desire to find salvation in "quelque antre" (*I,* v. 25) far from the iniquities of Paris tends to trivialize the solemnity of the devotional impulse, as does the speaker's devotion to Saint Molière in *Satire II.* Obvious examples of instinctual, natural behaviors—the racehorse in *Satire IV,* the barking dog in *Satire VII,* the ant and the jackass of *Satire VIII*—represent an authenticity, a standard of truth that transcends reason's capacity to dictate alternative behaviors. In his deviations from the idyllic Golden Age as imagined in *Satire V,* man has become the hollow, smug, ignoble creature that the *Satires* so adroitly particularize for the reader.

More important than the generalized notion of *la grande nature* as source of truth in the *Satires* is the individual's awareness of and fidelity to his or her own nature. For the *libertins,* one's "nature" was an infallible guide, an inner voice dictating behavior. Too often, however, social pressures to conform suppress this predetermined, instinctive force. As Antoine Adam demonstrates in his classic work on *libertinage,* Théophile de Viau made explicit reference to the cultivation of the *moi* in a number of his poems. For our purposes, the most notable is his *Satyre première,* echoes of which can be found, and not coincidentally, in Boileau's *Satire VIII.* In the conclusion Théophile's speaker's credo subscribes wholeheartedly to the *culte du moi:*

> Je croy que les destins ne font venir personne
> En l'estre des mortels qui n'ait l'ame assez bonne,
> Mais on la vient corrompre, et le celeste feu
> Qui luit à la raison ne nous dure que peu:
> Car l'imitation rompt nostre bonne trame,
> Et tousjours chez autruy fait demeurer nostre ame.
> Je pense que chacun aroit assez d'esprit,
> Suivant le libre train que Nature prescrit.
> A qui ne sçait farder, ny le cœur, ny la face,
> L'impertinence mesme a souvent bonne grace:
> Qui suivra son Genie, et gardera sa foy,
> Pour vivre bien-heureux, il vivra comme moy.
>
> (vv. 169–80)[5]

The speaker's evolution in the course of the *Satires* from engaged, free-spirited satirist to circumspect observer mirrors the quandary of the "second-stage" *libertin* as described in Claude Reichler's *L'Age libertin.* In his view early freethinkers such as Théophile de Viau misunderstood the unyielding strength of established social tenets and norms in their confrontations with officially sanctioned centers of power. The unfortunate fate of many early, defiant *libertins* convinced those who followed to conceal their system of beliefs behind the discreet facade of the *libertin honnête.* Playing a social role in accordance with permissible opinions, this individual simultaneously preserved his or her own intellectual and emotional autonomy. This "new" *libertin* thus obeyed the dictates of public order while at the same time assuring his liberty of personal judgment, thus reconciling inner conscience and outer comfort. Reichler adds that this retrenchment does not necessarily imply abdication, since in essence the *libertin honnête* chooses *freely* to lend his social self to others in daily discourse. While the speaker's obdurate resistance to this solution would lead apparently to social nullity, on the other hand inordinate respect for social representations would tend to abrogate the individual's singularity:

> le sujet est pris dans une double impasse. Soit, développant un imaginaire de la maîtrise, il nie à l'espace social sa précellence et refuse aux représentations collectives leurs fonctions configurantes; soit, envahi par les rôles qu'il avait cru simuler et animer, il est nié comme instance préservée et autonome, menacé de n'être qu'un répertoire de *dramatis personae*, de *caractères* du théâtre social. (Reichler 38)

The story of Boileau's speaker is one of continual tension between innate desires and inclinations and extrinsic commands to adjust these desires and inclinations in conformity to social custom and belief. For example, this lonely battle is concretized in *Satire III,* in which the speaker stands apart from the ravenous mob that embodies, at least in his mind, execrable taste. From the host's and guests' viewpoint, however, the speaker's sentiments would certainly represent a snobbish ingrate's peevish rant. By turning *Satire III* on its head, then, we not only see the speaker's struggle as extraordinarily difficult, but also appreciate the strength of his Muse and the Esprit—his own nature—that reign within him and drive him to satirize. As is most often the case among satirists, he depicts his plight as an unequal conflict matching a lone champion (Molière in *Satire II,* for example) in opposition to a well-organized army arrayed against him. Indeed, *Satire IV* suggests that all of mankind is the adversary. In this light, Boileau's early *Satires* emerge as much more than a critique of man and his social mores, but rather as a portrayal of the individual's struggle to realize his innermost needs and aspirations.

As revealed in *Satires VII* and *IX,* the persona's true contentment arises from easy-flowing verse that squarely strikes its target, effectively debasing, if not destroying, any affront to his moral, aesthetic, or social sensibilities. Not surprisingly, the inner pleasure derived from this activity does not rely on external approbation. Detached from worldly ambitions, the persona must nonetheless contend with competing elements in his psyche (e.g., the allegorical Raison) that pressure his natural

Esprit to adapt to outside expectations. This Epicurean notion of inner satisfaction does not, of course, have anything to do with Christian asceticism (associated with Damon in *Satire I*), hence the speaker's attraction to sensory delights in *Satire III* and to Paris and all that it represents, despite its many nuisances as outlined in *Satire VI,* for example. The speaker's Esprit does not hesitate to scorn the established dogmas that lie at the core of seventeenth-century French society. His refusal to forsake his personal viewpoints in the *Discours au Roy* is strong evidence—even in a satirist—of an intense desire for independence. In declining to kowtow to Louis XIV in the manner of the numerous poetic sycophants who surround the young king, the speaker preserves his own voice, even at the risk of being castigated as an insolent fool. This substantial risk, however, does not intimidate Esprit. Moreover, in *Satire V* his angry denunciation of the counterfeit aristocrat whose life dishonors his admirable ancestors proclaims a character unafraid of the consequences of condemning the powerful. The ongoing debate between the reality principle and the pleasure principle within the persona bears witness to the dangers that such boldness occasions. Yet Esprit insists that his *inner nature* dictates his tenacity and courage. To deny that nature would be to circumscribe one's self, to reduce oneself to a parody by attempting to imitate and to satisfy external expectations.

But the external forces against self-realization are powerful indeed. A writer confronted with a malicious, influential group of readers (who in this case may be writers as well, thereby strengthening their public credibility) who may willfully choose to reconstruct the author's works so that he appears to sneer at objects of collective reverence, i.e., Louis XIV, places that writer in an untenable position. However heartfelt the speaker's professions of sincerity might be, they would appear hollow if interpreted ironically, a real possibility given the context of the rest of his work. A poet confronted with a host of bad-faith readers finds himself in a troublesome predicament. The fact that Raison, a crucial element within the speaker's very own psyche, is apt to make significant misreadings (as in *Satire IX,* vv. 294–96), emphasizes the probability of textual distortions, whether intended or not. Errors by the donkey-eared segment of the audience are quite different, however, from flagrant and deliberate misreading. Silence, or at least a decisive *changement de style,* would be the sole defense against such an attack. For this reason the speaker's implicit withdrawal at the close of *Satire IX*—and in reality Nicolas Boileau-Despréaux's shift from satire to *épître*—might be justified inasmuch as spiteful misinterpretation constitutes an artistic impasse for the serious writer. A poet who cannot connect with his readers, for whatever reason, is mute. Despite the intense personal pleasure that skewering fools affords him, a modicum of public approbation, along with basic social ambitions, motivate the persona in the *Satires.*[6] Unknown future readers may rehabilitate him, but the Epicurean speaker cannot retreat, Damon-like, from the world. In *Satire I* Damon's bitter renunciation of Paris—a metonym for the reading public—underscores the importance of the *raté*'s fate as a cautionary example for the brash speaker of the *Discours au Roy* who plays the effaced role of neutral presenter and presumed listener in *Satire I.* The poem suggests that even the most talented of writers (it is not certain whether Damon fits this category!) can go unappreciated by an indifferent, undiscerning, or corrupt audience. The poet's life provides little stability, and he who trusts to the good taste of his readers will likely suffer Damon's fate. The satirist thus finds himself in a *huis clos:* the dull society that he so loathes is also the audience for his verse, as well as the mine of inspiration that drives him to write. We can infer Boileau's mistrust of his audience at this point in his career in the *Discours sur la satire,* a brief prose apology that was printed in 1668 with *Satire IX*, which first appeared separately from the other *Satires.* Boileau ponders why "lay" readers would side with the aggrieved—and far from silent—writers targeted in his *Satires:*

> Mais j'avoüe que j'ay esté un peu surpris du chagrin bizarre de certains Lecteurs, qui, au lieu de se divertir d'une querelle du Parnasse, dont ils pouvoient estre spectateurs indifferens, ont mieux aimé prendre parti, et s'affliger avec les Ridicules, que de se réjoüir avec les honnestes gens. (*Œuvres complètes,* ed. Boudhors 1:77)[7]

To cling doggedly to satire, therefore, however pleasurable for the writer, will eventually destroy him. As Raison reminds Esprit in *Satire IX,* he must conform and adapt to this public if he is to avoid Damon's forced retreat to the *désert.*

A ray of hope sparkles, however, when the speaker contemplates the divine Molière, patron saint of *la rime,* in *Satire II.* While the speaker's prayer to Saint Molière at the close of this poem appears ironically to assert his feigned desire to retreat from satire, it effectively prefigures the real withdrawal of *Satire IX.* In opposition to the penitent Damon who flees the world in order to save his soul, the speaker creates a kind of secular cult in which the true believer consecrates his life to *la rime,* which of course must be worshiped in Paris. The speaker's rare good taste permits him to distinguish between Molière the unique artist and the legion of happy but fatuous poetasters that proliferate in the capital. Upheld and defended against bad taste and its innumerable minions by lonely champions such as the messiah/Molière on the most exalted level and the disciple/speaker below him, the battle of good taste vs. bad taste receives full burlesque treatment in the famous *repas ridicule.*

Despite the speaker's fortunate escape from the inferno of bad taste depicted in *Satire III,* it is not surprising that his fellow guests appear to savor all the bad "tastes" offered to them; they enjoy themselves immensely, presumably even during the conventional drunken brawl near the poem's conclusion. A fundamental theme of the *Satires,* the speaker's inability to achieve the Epicurean's prime goal of realizing inner felicity, is a dominant element in his indictment of reason in *Satire IV.* The *libertin*'s mistrust of reason receives eloquent articulation in this poem dedicated to universal folly. The speaker's daunting realization that Queen Reason (and thus good taste) may not be the unerring, all-powerful mentor to which he unquestionably adheres in *Satires II* and *III* does not, however, obliterate his trust in her. The matter of the ensuing *Satire V*—the nurturing strength of prior example, of illustrious models who acted in accordance with reason's dictates—motivates the speaker to fight on against the forces of dullness arrayed against him. While intimating that the efforts of the poet/satirist to undo the negative examples that undermine the very foundations of civilized society are nothing less than nobly heroic, a now familiar obstacle reappears in *Satire VI* to confound the speaker in his holy war against his outside enemies and their allies, his inner demons.

The persona's persistent castigation of Paris and all that it represents enhances the *cour-ville* dichotomy that provides transition between *Satires V* and *VI.* Extending the literal concept of space and locale evoked in this duality is the speaker's metaphorical quest for an aesthetic "site" that will award him the emotional serenity for which he so ardently yearns.[8] His literal and figurative longing for a sanctuary where he might "Aller entretenir ses douces rêveries" (*VI,* v. 124) becomes in *Satire VII* a one-sided debate over which *generic* lodging—*laudatio* or *vituperatio?*—would offer him the most physical and spiritual contentment. Practically settled even before it begins, this debate underscores the theme of personal *manie* (also conveyed through a "lodging" metaphor in *Satire IV*—the "Petites-Maisons" of the mind [v. 4]) as supreme authority governing the individual's needs, desires, ambitions, and actions. The ensuing *Satire VIII* establishes itself as an effort to arrive at first principles concerning man's true nature, a "rebeginning" (cf. *VII,* v. 96), a kind of public legalistic hearing, as opposed to the interior dialogue of *Satire VII,* which leaves no doubt as to man's essential folly. The speaker's smart-ass spokes"person" who adjudicates the debate in favor of mankind's lunacy provokes the vehement reaction of Raison in *Satire IX.*

Although the continuing dispute between Raison and Esprit still appears to be tilted heavily in favor of the latter's arguments in *Satire IX,* Esprit is finally won over (silenced) only when pragmatic Raison turns the discussion to the subject of the King, with whom of course the *Satires* began in the form of the *Discours au Roy.* As ultimate—divine—authority (*Discours,* vv. 3–4), Louis incarnates for Esprit the sole truly legitimate subject to which he can in good conscience address his verse, since the King, unlike the rest of the audience, is certain to comprehend and appreciate his work in the spirit in which it was created. The ideal reader, Louis is incapable of *mauvaise foi.* By abandoning satire and shifting to an unspecified, but more favorable "stile," which may illuminate (however feebly) royal glory, the speaker will possibly realize the artistic *and* material felicity that at least a part of him craves. This state of contentment differs in degree and in kind from the luxuriant, but solitary, pleasure that skewering fools affords him. Inner satisfaction must make way for a contentment that derives from outside approval as well.

The image of the King as ultimate exemplum was punctuated at the beginning of the early *Satires* in the *Discours au*

Roy, at the midpoint in *Satire V,* and at the very end in the closing verses of *Satire IX.* Louis XIV thus emerges as a recurring *point de repère* who appropriates to himself the good sense, taste, honor, perspicacity, constraint, and virtue that the speaker finds so rare in the world (i.e., Paris) in which he moves. Just as the persona's satiric forebears provide indispensable guidance and reassurance in the family of satirical poets, the King is the ideal model in the much broader family of man. By seeing Louis as a potential corrective to the dullness surrounding him, the speaker can at the very least rationalize a change in *stile.* Instead of a series of courageous but lonely, witty but ineffectual, tirades aimed at a multitude of uncomprehending personal and abstract antagonists—and despite the private fulfillment, albeit fleeting, that this affords him—the speaker looks to the King as a means of resisting his adversaries more effectively. In rededicating himself to the King, the speaker might reconcile and eventually harmonize the heretofore incompatible forces of personal happiness and self-respect that war within his psyche, as depicted, for example, in *Satires II* and *IV.*

The speaker's opening gambit to Louis in *Epistre I* demonstrates remarkable articulation with *Satire IX.* Here he plainly declares the new direction established at the close of the debate between Raison and Esprit. Despite this revitalized devotion to the King, the customary hesitations, the horror of gross blunders in this "new" genre of the epistle, seemingly betray the same conflicted personality at work:

> GRAND ROY, c'est vainement qu'abjurant la Satire,
> Pour Toy seul desormais j'avois fait vœu d'écrire.
> Dés que je prens la plume, Apollon éperdu
> Semble me dire: "Arreste, insensé, que fais-tu?
> Sçais tu dans quels perils aujourd'huy tu t'engages?
> Cette mer où tu cours est celebre en naufrages."
> (*Epistre I,* vv. 1–6)

Transparent allusions to the preceding *Satire IX* accompany equally distinct echoes of the concluding verses of the *Discours au Roy,* with the speaker's comic return to shipwreck imagery. This diffident overture advances slowly, as the speaker revives the recurrent themes of facile elegists and his nightmare of writing equally loathsome poetry for a nonexistent audience in this unfamiliar and demanding genre. These fears dissipate, however, as the poem progresses from initial doubt to a more confident voice as it gradually shifts into the epistle mode. True to its genre, *Epistre I* reflects upon a moral precept with a specific addressee in an entertaining, lighthearted fashion. Although satirical barbs abound, the speaker's cheerful, but quite serious, counsel to Louis XIV about the blessings of peace clearly reveals this prescriptive purpose.[9] In a recent article Wood has explored the generic distinctions between the *Satires* and the *Epistres.* Accentuating the Horatian impulse at work and Boileau's apparent ambition to become the French Horace, Wood also notes the new emphasis on *laudatio* at the expense of *vituperatio*, a less strident tone, and a reluctance to name names, despite the frequent satiric jabs in the *Epistres.*[10]

Composed in 1674, the speaker's meditations on self-knowledge and wisdom in *Epistre V* explicitly reconfirm the move away from trenchant literary satire disclosed in *Satire IX.* The speaker's supposed doubt as to whether he should return to satire's "plaisantes malices" (v. 5) in the first verses—formulated as mock-serious questions to his addressee Guilleragues, "maistre en l'art de plaire" (v. 1)—disguises his real concerns centering on moral edification. *Satire IX*'s staid and pragmatic Raison undoubtedly motivates the speaker's new quest:

> Je ne sens plus l'aigreur de ma bile premiere,
> Et laisse aux froids Rimeurs une libre carriere.
> Ainsi donc Philosophe à la Raison soûmis,
> Mes defauts desormais sont mes seuls ennemis.
> C'est l'erreur que je fuis; c'est la vertu que j'aime.
> Je songe à me connoistre, et me cherche en moi-même.
> (*Epistre V,* vv. 21–26)

The speaker's cautionary meditation on the disparity between lucre and felicity leads to his respectful gratitude for the King's recent generosity (who "Creut voir dans ma franchise un merite inconnu, / Et d'abord de ses dons enfla mon revenu" [vv. 127–28]).[11] In light of the manifest fear of poverty expressed in many of the early *Satires,* this financial boon vindicates Raison's pragmatic arguments for a change in "stile" in *Satire IX.*[12] While the speaker has eluded—at least temporarily—the impecunious fate of the archetypal poetic failure Damon, he has not achieved the Epicurean inner tranquillity so sought after in the *Satires.* That goal remains ever elusive, dependent as it is upon composing "vers immortels" (v. 140) that can "satisfaire mon cœur" (v. 144).

In the end, this is the objective that the speaker sets for himself in the early *Satires*. Although his witty, explicit, sometimes harsh, jabs directed at mankind's foibles—in particular those related to contemporary writers and the reading public—have from the first attracted the attention of readers both amateur and professional, the speaker's evolving quest for contentment and self-understanding transcends his attacks on dullness. Profoundly linked to a literary vocation obsessively examined and pursued, the speaker's journey of discovery points inward, not outward: the early *Satires* weave a complex account of an individual's attempts to probe the nature of self and its interactions with the external world. When read and analyzed as a coherent work within a self-referential context, the first nine *Satires* and the *Discours au Roy* exhibit a lyrical impulse. Boileau desired to record in his poetry not only his sincere attitudes and opinions, but more importantly the inner turmoil, fears, pleasures, and ambitions of a poet in the age of Louis XIV. As a relatively well-known literary figure becoming established as the 1660s progressed, he was obliged to adapt to the exigencies that royal favor implied in the reign of Louis XIV. His first collection of poetry records the beginnings of his journey from *jeune dogue* to historiographer to the King.

Notes

Introduction

1. See Charles Révillout, "La Légende de Boileau," and René Bray, *La Formation de la doctrine classique.* Sima Godfrey, "The Anxiety of Anticipation: Ulterior Motives in French Poetry," has pondered the "effet Boileau" on the history of French poetry. In her assessment, inspired by Harold Bloom's *The Anxiety of Influence,* the evolution of French poetry is marked by epic critics, among whom Boileau stands as the "paradigmatic example" (6). Unlike the English tradition, in which individual poets, in their attempts to "rewrite" the poems of their predecessors, engage in an Oedipal dialogue with the paternal "strong" figures of the past, the French tradition requires poets to rewrite not Boileau's individual poems, but rather the canonical prestige and theoretical authority that the "législateur du Parnasse" embodies in the *Art poétique.* This exalted image of Boileau as father figure that all French poets since foster within them does not, however, address the question of why it was *Boileau*'s "art poétique," and not another, that created this fixation on poetics rather than poems. The fact that the doctrine did not pass on to future generations in a form other than the verses of the *Art poétique* suggests that Boileau's talent as a *poet* might have led to his eventual status as institution.

2. Gustave Lanson, *Boileau.* See also Daniel Mornet, *Nicolas Boileau;* Pierre Clarac, *Boileau;* R. Bray, *Boileau, l'homme et l'œuvre;* H. E. White, Jr., *Nicolas Boileau.* For an excellent history of Boileau's literary fortune, see Bernard Beugnot and Roger Zuber, *Boileau: Visages anciens, visages nouveaux, 1665–1970.*

3. Allen G. Wood, "Boileau and Affective Response," has elucidated the emotional element in Boileau.

4. E. B. O. Borgerhoff, "Boileau Satirist *Animi Gratia.*"

5. Wood, "The *Regent du Parnasse* and *Vraisemblance.*"

6. Nathan Edelman, "*L'Art poétique:* 'Longtemps plaire et jamais ne lasser.'"

7. Cleanth Brooks, *The Well Wrought Urn.*

8. Several prior critics have accepted *a priori* that the *Satires* constitute an entity. The excellent article by Susan Tiefenbrun, "Boileau and His Friendly Enemy: A Poetics of Satiric Criticism," is most remarkable in this regard. Simone Ackerman, "Les *Satires* de Boileau: Un Théâtre de l'absurde avant la lettre," likens the *Satires* to absurdist theatre. For Ackerman, Boileau depicts a random universe in opposition to the seventeenth-century theoreticians' belief in an ideal of beauty, a preordained design that the artist must strive to achieve.

9. A notable exception is *The Ladder of Higher Designs: Structure and Interpretation of the French Lyric Sequence,* ed. Doranne Fenoaltea and David Lee Rubin.

10. See Miner 18–43.

11. See Barbara Herrnstein Smith, *Poetic Closure: A Study of How Poems End,* for a presentation of structural integrative principles.

12. The bibliography on this subject is substantial. For a useful summary, see Susan H. Braund's bibliography in her *Roman Verse Satire.* In genres other than satire, Virgil's *Eclogues* has often been cited as a book for which the poet intended a perceivable structure. See, for example, J. Van Sickle, *The Design of Virgil's Bucolics.* In the case of Horace, see Matthew S. Santirocco, *Unity and Design in Horace's Odes.*

13. "I think that there can be little question that Horace has given careful thought to the order of his Satires and organized a book that makes sense of his definition of satire as a thoughtful combination of nondoctrinaire Epicurean ethics and of poetic techniques and purposes. Three interrelated groups of three poems expose us by different methods to the satirist as poet-moralist (or moralist-poet), and the final poem makes clear how confident and committed Horace the poet wishes to appear" (Anderson 61). See also David Armstrong, *Horace,* and a series of articles by C. A. Van Rooy, "Arrangement and Structure of Satires in Horace."

14. Notable exceptions are two exceptional contributions to Boileau scholarship: Borgerhoff's article "Boileau Satirist *Animi Gratia,*" which centers on a reading of *Satire IX,* taking into account its crucial placement in the corpus of the satires: "Thus the whole poem has to read in the light of the previous satires, indeed in the light of Boileau's whole career in the literary world up to this time" (246). Borgerhoff's intention, however, is not to examine how *Satire IX* integrates into the ensemble we call the *Satires.* Susan Tiefenbrun's article "Boileau and His Friendly Enemy: A Poetics of Satiric Criticism," examines the twelve *Satires,* the *Discours au Roy,* the prose preface, and the two prose *Discours,* "With special attention to its unity of form and content" (673). Ackerman, "Les *Satires* de Boileau," accepts as a given that the *Satires* are an entity whose structure approximates that of the absurdist theater (see note 8 above). In Régnier studies, Katherine Lawrence has analyzed cyclical rhetorical patterns in her holistic study of Boileau's influential predecessor: "Rhetorical and Fictional Aspects in the *Satyres* of Mathurin Régnier."

15. The true chronological order of the poems has been fairly well established. Georges Ascoli, *Boileau, Satires de I à IX* (3), reproduces the order given by Boileau in notes added to Pierre Le Verrier's commentary (early 1700s) of the *Satires:*

—*I* and *VI* were originally one satire, composed around 1657;

—*VII,* 1660–61;

—*II, IV, V,* 1663–64;

—the *Discours au Roy,* 1662–64;

—*III,* between 1664 and 1666;

—*IX* (here there is some confusion; Boileau's friend and commentator Le Verrier gives the dates as 1662–63, but Ascoli prefers the date posited by another friend and admirer, Claude Brossette's 1667;

—*VIII,* after all the others, probably 1667.

According to this schema, the real order of composition would thus be: *I, VI, VII, II, IV, V, III, IX, VIII.* It is impossible to know where to place the *Discours au Roy.* In his edition Charles-H. Boudhors (1: 175) refers to a note by Boileau himself placed in Le Verrier's commentary on the 1701 edition intimating, ambiguously ("l'ordre dans lequel elles doivent être placées"), that the poems should be positioned according to this chronological sequence. It is interesting to note that this apparent decree was never obeyed in *any* published edition. The first authorized edition of the *Satires* was published in 1666, with the following order: *I–V, Discours au Roy, VI–VII.* The second authorized edition of the *Satires* (1667) places the *Discours au Roy* in the lead position, followed by *I–VII* in that order. The first volume containing all of *Satires I–IX* appeared in 1668: *Discours au Roy, I–IX, Discours sur la Satire.* After 1694 *Satires X* and *XI* appeared in all editions. In 1701 there appeared the *Œuvres diverses* (Boileau's "édition favorite"), with a *Préface générale. Satire XII,* which dates from 1705, was published apart from the other satires in 1711, and was included with the other eleven poems only in the 1716 edition, five years after his death.

16. Adam, *Les Premières Satires de Boileau* 10. The Arsenal manuscript allowed Adam and others to reproduce the chronological order of that manuscript, which he believed was accurate. The sole exception concerns *Satires II* and *VII,* which apparently were written simultaneously, although published on different dates. The manuscript places *II* before *VII,* but Adam concludes that events indicate that *VII* was completed before *II.*

17. ". . . si l'on admet que les *Satires* sont d'abord des instruments de polémique, leur forme la plus intéressante n'est pas celle que l'auteur leur a donnée quand se furent dissipées les passions d'une lutte furieuse" (9). In his excellent study *Boileau and the Nature of Neo-Classicism,* Gordon Pocock also examines the *Satires* in the probable order of their composition. Like Adam, Pocock's objective is not a structural and thematic integration of the individual poems, but rather focuses on Boileau's treatment of classical precepts.

Chapter One
The *Discours au Roy:* Conflicted Beginnings

1. It is interesting to note that Régnier's 1608 edition, which, including the *Discours au Roy,* contained ten satires, and apparently was the only edition in which the poet took an active personal interest. Posthumous editions of Régnier's work do not respect the author's prescribed sequence. See Régnier xxiii.

2. "Satiriser, n'est-ce pas critiquer, moquer, railler, contester donc un ordre que d'autres acceptent ou révèrent?" (B. Bray 266; see also Pineau 225–27). Régnier was also well aware of the satirist's predicament in his own *Discours.* Although his speaker defends satire's inherent temerity and ponders briefly the clash of *laudatio* and *vituperatio,* Régnier remains less daring than Boileau in his relatively mild criticisms of his rival, self-serving poets:

> Mais, Sire, c'est un vol bien eslevé pour ceux
> Qui foibles d'exercice et d'esprit paresseux,
> Enorgueillis d'audace en leur barbe premiere
> Chanterent ta valeur d'une façon grossiere,
> Trahissant tes honneurs avecq' la vanité
> D'attenter par ta gloire à l'immortalité.
>
> (vv. 97–102)

3. Rubin argues that in many of his poems La Fontaine uses parody, allusion, and dialectical imagery to suggest his own reservations concerning Louis XIV's true glory. See "Icon and Caricature: Poetic Images of the Sun King."

4. Unless otherwise noted, all quotes from Boileau are taken from the Charles-H. Boudhors's edition of the *Œuvres complètes.* The *Discours* and all *Satires* are from the first volume; the *Epistres* are from volume 2. I have also consulted, and occasionally quoted from (with appropriate reference), Françoise Escal's Pléiade edition of Boileau's works.

5. "A la mort de Mazarin en mars 1661, Louis XIV fit savoir à son entourage qu'il entendait désormais gouverner personnellement, sans premier ministre" (Escal, in her ed. of Boileau, *Œuvres complètes* 864).

6. Horace's words in *Epistles* II.1.1–4 to Caesar Augustus no doubt take the lead here: "Cum tot sustineas et tant negotia solus . . ." ("Seeing that you alone carry the weight of so many great charges . . ." [*Satires, Epistles,* trans. Fairclough]). All Latin quotes from Horace are from *Satires, Epistles,* trans. Fairclough. Translations will be identified.

7. Among the several, sometimes assimilated, characters in mythology called Argos, the two most significant are the hundred-eyed figure whose various adventures point up his unceasing vigilance, and the builder of the *Argo,* the ship that carried Jason and the Argonauts, including Argos, in their quest for the Golden Fleece.

8. Conversely, Frye broadly describes panegyric thus: "In the panegyric the poet invites his reader to gaze with him at something else" (295). Indeed, of the three forms of oratory discourse, Aristotelian poetics describes the panegyric as a demonstrative, or epideictic, genre. It shares with judiciary (the lawyer's) and deliberative (the politician's) discourse an identical enunciative structure, "linking the person who speaks to the person he is speaking to and both of them to a subject about whom the locutor speaks to the allocutee" (Marin 48). In each form, however, the effect on the auditor varies. In panegyric, "the auditor is spectator, he 'contemplates' the speech being given 'theoretically,' and when he judges, he does not pronounce himself on what is said but on the potential (the talent) of the person speaking, not on the content of the speech but on the way in which it is given" (49).

9. Pocock has pointed out the underlying play of opposites in the *Discours au Roy:* "The style is a mixture of the styles considered appropriate by neo-classical theory: the *style pompeux* for panegyric, and the more familiar style for satire" (39–40).

10. Poetry of attack and poetry of celebration—satire and panegyric—constitute antinomical genres, although they both engage in subjects that may seem quite significant when they first appear, but whose force may diminish as time passes and the topicality of their objects fades.

11. The reader hardly need be reminded of King Midas's wish for any object he touched to turn to gold, which of course became a nightmare, and Icarus's foolhardy flight, which resulted in the sun's rays melting his waxed wings and his subsequent fall to earth. In his first satire, *Au roy,* Régnier exploited the same well-worn metaphor of the poet's soaring inspiration with an intent similar to Boileau's speaker's protest that his Muse is unequal to the task at hand:

> Mais, Sire, c'est un vol bien eslevé pour ceux
> Qui foibles d'exercice et d'esprit paresseux,
> Enorgueillis d'audace en leur barbe premiere
> Chanterent ta valeur d'une façon grossiere.
> (vv. 97–100)

12. In strictly historical terms, the sovereign's "absolute individuality" within his realm would make Boileau's possible *rapprochement* with the King extremely presumptuous, even dangerous. See Baglioli 206.

13. In his *Traité de la poésie française,* Father Mourgues defines the eclogue thus:

> . . . un ouvrage de Poésie, où l'on fait parler des Bergers, ou des gens oisifs avec des termes naturels, et des pensées naïves, comme ont fait Théocrite, Virgile, Vida, Sannazar, et quelques autres, tant anciens que modernes. Son style doit être moins orné qu'élégant; les images riantes; les comparaisons tirées des choses les plus communes; les sentiments tendres et délicats; le tour simple; la cadence modérée. (266; qtd. in Saisselin 73)

14. Horace, *Epistles* II.1.237–40: "idem rex ille, poema / qui tam ridiculum tam care prodigus emit, / edicto vetuit, ne quis se praeter Apellen / pingeret . . ." ("That same king who lavishly paid so dearly for a poem so foolish, by an edict forbade anyone save Apelles to paint him . . ." [*Satires, Epistles,* trans. Fairclough]).

15. The notion of generic heritage presents itself here if we look at a possible allusion to Horace, *Satires* II.1.28–34, in which the speaker declares his intent to follow the traces of Lucilius: "ille velut fidis arcana sodalibus olim / credebat libris, neque si male cesserat, usquam / decurrens alio, neque si bene" (vv. 30–32, "Long ago he made his books his faithful friends and to them / trusted his most private thoughts. In good fortune and bad, / he never rushed to other confidants" [*Satires and Epistles,* trans. Fuchs]). Poetry as repository for the poet's inner thoughts and feelings was of course in vogue among Renaissance poets. Du Bellay's sonnet from his *Antiquités de Rome,* "Je ne veulx point fouiller au sein de la nature," is perhaps the best-known example of the theme.

Boileau's v. 71 portends *Satire IV*'s reference to the satirist's commitment to stringent soul-searching:

> Le plus sage est celui qui ne pense point l'estre.
> Qui toûjours pour un autre est enclin vers la douceur,
> Se regarde soi-mesme en severe Censeur.
>
> (vv. 54–56)

16. A conventional symbol for diligence, the bee takes on additional symbolic connotations in its various mythological and legendary incarnations. Most appropriate for Boileau's purposes is the bee as a representation of intelligence, poetry, and eloquence, as in the legends of Plato and Pindar, on whose lips bees landed as they slumbered in their cradles. Boileau's vv. 74–75 call to mind Théophile de Viau's "Le Matin," vv. 13–16:

> Déjà la diligente avette
> Boit la marjolaine et le thym,
> Et revient riche du butin
> Qu'elle a pris sur le mont Hymette.
>
> (*Œuvres poétiques,* ed. Saba 51)

17. See the important Borgerhoff work *The Freedom of French Classicism* 204–12. Interestingly, Boileau's vv. 77–80 bring to mind lines from "Élégie à une dame," the program poem of one of his signal "victims," Théophile de Viau, vv. 116–19:

> Diversement je laisse et reprends mon sujet,
> Mon âme imaginant n'a point la patience
> De bien polir les vers et ranger la science:
> La règle me déplaît, j'écris confusément.
>
> (*Œuvres poétiques,* ed. Saba 105)

18. Ascoli's note emphasizes extratextual evidence for Boileau's explicit reference to the *Tartuffe* controversy:

> Très adroitement, Boileau laisse entendre que les ennemis de ses Satires, sont les mêmes hommes qui se sont affirmés ennemis de Molière et de Tartufe; c'est habile, car il sait que le Roi a nettement pris parti pour Molière, s'il a temporairement accordé aux dévots l'interdiction de la pièce. (18)

19. V. 58: "Pour chanter un Auguste, il faut estre un Virgile" further invalidates the impact of panegyric. The analogy between Louis and

Caesar Augustus does not necessarily imply that present-day Virgils, who, after all, are extraordinarily *rare* poetic geniuses, can revitalize the genre.

20. See Fowler 191–212 for an analysis of generic modulation.

21. Brody devotes several valuable pages to Boileau's use of the ancient motif of the poet as traveler in his *Boileau and Longinus* 59–61.

Chapter Two
Two Poetic Paradigms

1. See Tiefenbrun 675.

2. See also Susan H. Braund, "City and Country in Roman Satire."

3. See Louis A. MacKenzie, Jr., "Three Literary Visions of Seventeenth-Century Paris."

4. The depravity of the big city and the desire to flee into the "wilderness" of course recurs as a theme throughout world literature. Horace's Sabine farm and his elegy on country life in the *Satires* II.6 is notable in this regard. See also Highet, *Juvenal the Satirist: A Study* 64–68. In seventeenth-century French poetry two prominent examples, among many, are François de Maynard's ode "Alcipe, reviens dans nos bois" and Racan's *Stances sur la retraite.* Huppert discusses the sociological and historical reasons for this state of mind in sixteenth- and seventeenth-century France in his *Les Bourgeois Gentilshommes* (162–70).

5. Régnier's third satire, also inspired by Juvenal, repeats many of the Roman satirist's themes. This monologue, however, deletes explicit reference to the city as source of social ills, neither does the speaker specifically condemn, nor express a wish to desert, the metropolis. Régnier's *Satire II* also contains a fierce reaction to the fate of the unappreciated poet in a society of Philistines.

6. The passionately immoderate views of Umbricius contribute to his ambivalence. For more on the speaker in Juvenal, see Martin M. Winkler, *The Persona in Three Satires of Juvenal.*

7. See Normand Doirion, "Le Pauvre Poète: De la censure des mœurs parisiennes à la sublimation esthétique"; Aulotte 56–58; John Lough, *Writers and Public in France.*

8. On the other hand, Wood argues in his "Boileau, l'équivoque, et l'œuvre ouverte" that the poet deliberately downplays irony in order to minimize ambiguity: "L'ironie risque de laisser errer les lecteurs moins avisés qui ne comprennent pas l'inversion entre l'intention et l'expression. Pour cette raison, les passages ironiques sont souvent annoncés explicitement comme tels dans les *Satires.* . . . Ce n'est pas un principe qui structure les *Satires* et exige une lecture constamment antiphrastique du propos" (280).

9. Perhaps the most popular of Counter-Reformation penitents who retreated from the urban world (in this case Marseilles) to find salvation in a primeval grotto was the reformed prostitute Mary Magdalene. French seventeenth-century literature offers many imitators of the Magdalene legend. See, for example, Wolfgang Leiner, "Métamorphoses magdaléennes."

10. A line lifted from Juvenal (*Satire III,* v. 41): "Quid Romae faciam?" (What am I doing in Rome?).

11. "It is easier for a camel to go through the eye of a needle, than for a rich man to enter into the kingdom of God" (Mark 10.25).

12. It is interesting to note that an older (and wiser?) speaker celebrated the peace of the countryside in the *Epistre VI.* The antipathy toward Paris expressed in this poem echoes Damon as well as the disgruntled speaker of *Satire VI, l'embarras de Paris:* "Qu'heureux est le Mortel, qui du monde ignoré, / Vit content de soi-mesme en un coin retiré!" (*Epistre VI,* vv. 99–100).

13. Doirion has also remarked on the contrasts between the *pauvre poète* Damon and Molière.

14. It hardly need be said that scholars have speculated on the real identity of Damon. See, for example, Adam, *Les Premières Satires de Boileau* 131–32, and Boudhors, in his ed. of Boileau, *Œuvres complètes* 1: 188–92.

15. It should be remembered that seventeenth-century usage conferred a much broader meaning on the word *rime:* "verse compositions." See Brody, *Boileau and Longinus* 63.

16. See Pocock 35: "We may wonder whether Boileau's sympathy with Jansenism is not founded on an attitude evident in this poem: he and Molière are assumed to be the literary Elect."

17. In his *Satire XV,* Régnier also lambasted his tyrannical Muse and her incessant attacks on his reason.

18. See Kernan (3–5), who, inspired by Pope's *Dunciad,* uses this term to specify the targeted adversary of all literary satirists as "an ancient and powerful force operating constantly and expressing its own nature through all lands and times" (3). Pope of course described this force more poetically: "Still her old Empire to restore she tries, / For, born a Goddess, Dulness never dies" (*The Dunciad* 1.15–16).

19. All Latin quotes from Horace are from *Satires, Epistles,* trans. Fairclough. Translations will be identified.

> But anyone who wants to write an authentic poem
> needs an honest censor's soul as much as paper.
> He must be firm: words which lack sufficient dignity
> or don't make clear sense should not be circulated;
> so he'll throw them out . . .
> . . . .
> He cuts back wild growths, carefully smooths passages
> which seem too rough, takes out whatever has no strength.
> He seems to play, but really he works, like a dancer
> who's first a satyr on the stage, then a rustic Cyclops.
> I wouldn't mind being called lazy and sloppy
> if my bad work seemed good to me, or at least not bad:
> better than knowing and suffering.
> (Horace, *Epistles* II.2.109–13, 122–28,
> from *Satires and Epistles,* trans. Fuchs)

20. Boileau was also criticized for omitting the *ne* in the second hemistich of v. 62. See Ascoli 50.

21. See Hodgart 129:

> The device of the crowded canvas is found almost everywhere from Juvenal's *Rome* through Pope's *Dunciad* to the horrible collective canteens of *1984*. The reasons for its prevalence are that satire is an urban art, and that city crowds, mindless and faceless, *are* unpleasant to most people. But there is a deeper reason for the effectiveness of this device. The opposite of the satirist's butt is the heroic individual who in tragedy or epic is pictured as standing alone in his moment of triumph or defeat.

22. Wood, in his *Literary Satire and Theory: A Study of Horace, Boileau, and Pope,* has pointed out the three-tier configuration among satirical poets: "Although none of the personae in Boileau's literary satires pretends to rival Horace, Juvenal, or Molière, they are much further up the mountain than Pelletier, Scudéry, or Chapelain. Examples of poets at both extremes serve to situate clearly the persona and his poetic ability in each of the satires" (66). It should also be noted that the third classification would include as well those critics who maintained an undeviating hostility to Molière throughout his career. *Satire II*'s time of composition in itself would suggest in this regard Molière's relatively recent problems with the notorious *Tartuffe.*

23. In his *Boileau and Longinus,* Brody emphasizes Boileau's concept of *art* in the last four verses of *Satire II:*

> From Boileau's vantage point the *art* which Molière possessed was in reality a form of *génie,* in the modern sense. In a takeoff of his opening lines he had to conclude *Satire II* with the avowal that what he had wanted to learn from Molière was by its very nature unteachable. (73)

24. Boileau's choice of the name Damon emulates the practice of the Roman satirists to choose names for their symbolic significance. For example, Umbricius, in Juvenal's *Satire III,* evokes *umbra,* denoting "shadow" or "ghost." (See Braund, "City and Country in Roman Satire" 29.) The possible pun on *démon,* meaning a *mauvais génie,* adds thematic depth to *Satire I.* Other potential puns play on similar Latin words.

Chapter Three
Nourishing Literature: "De gustibus . . . est disputandum"

1. Tobin 1–18.

2. In his 1735 *Cuisiner moderne,* Vincent de la Chapelle echoes L. S. R. and thus confirms the triumph of *classicisme gastronomique:*

> Les arts ont des regles generales; ceux qui veulent les exercer doivent s'y conformer. Ces regles ne suffisent pourtant pas, & la perfection exige que l'on travaille sans cesse à renchérir sur une pratique constante, & cependant sujette, comme toute autre chose, à la vicissitude des tems. (Qtd. in preface to La Varenne, *Le Cuisinier françois* 19)

3. "But the banquet is even more important as the occasion for wise discourse, for the gay truth. There is an ancient tie between the feast and the spoken word" (Bakhtin 283). See Mikhail Bakhtin's chapter "Banquet Imagery in Rabelais" for a detailed analysis of this literary commonplace, in his *Rabelais and His World.*

4. See Nicholas Cronk, "The Singular Voice: Monologism and French Classical Discourse," for a Bakhtinian discussion of dialogism and monologism in seventeenth-century French literature.

5. Barbara Wheaton, *Savoring the Past: The French Kitchen and Table from 1300 to 1789,* provides a detailed description of seventeenth-century *bisque* (128). In his definition of *ortolan,* Furetière (*Dictionnaire universel*) adds: ". . . il s'engraisse extrêmément & est délicieux à manger." He qualifies *bisque* as a "Potage exquis & succulent fait de pigeons, poulets, béatilles, jus de mouton, & autres bons ingrediens."

6. Brillat-Savarin 37. See especially Roland Barthes's commentary in this edition, "Lecture de Brillat-Savarin," for an analysis of the semiotics of food. See also Barthes, "Toward a Psychosociology of Contemporary Food Consumption": "For what is food? It is not only a collection of products that can be used for statistical or nutritional studies. It is also, and at the same time, a system of communication, a body of images, a protocol of usages, situations, and behavior" (167).

7. Food as a marker of character has been a prevalent shorthand technique in French fiction. See, for example, Brown 15 ff.

8. See Edwin Duval's exemplary anaylsis of this poem in *Poesis and Poetic Tradition* (139–68).

9. Additional sources include Juvenal's *Satire VIII,* Petronius's "Banquet of Trimalchio" in his *Satyrica,* Furetière's *Satire IV,* "Déjeuner d'un Procureur," and Berni's third satire in his *Capitulo del prete da Povigliano.* See "The Horrible Party," in Highet, *Anatomy of Satire* 221–24; and Ulrich Schulz-Buschhaus, "Boileaus 'Repas ridicule,' Klassische Satire und burleske Poetologie." For more information on French predecessors, see Mornet, *Nicolas Boileau* 50–80.

10. Freudenberg 232–34.

11. Pineau 70–71. See also pp. 88–90 regarding Boileau's departure from prior French satire. Régnier was inspired by Horace, *Satires* I.9, and Caporali's *Del Pedante.*

12. Schulz-Buschhaus (75) sees a situation and character similar to Boileau's egregious host in Horace, *Satires* I.9.1, "Ibam forte Via Sacra . . ." ("I was strolling along the Sacred Way . . ." [*Satires, Epistles,* trans.

Fairclough]), in which a voluble boor importunes the peacefully strolling but hapless speaker.

13. Ascoli quotes the proverb "Jamais un bon coq ne fut gras" (58).

14. See, for example, Barthes in his ed. of Brillat-Savarin's *Physiologie du goût:*

> Cadmus, qui apporta l'écriture en Grèce, avait été le cuisinier du roi de Sidon. Donnons ce trait mythologique pour apologue au rapport qui unit le langage et la gastronomie. Ces deux puissances n'ont-elles pas le même organe? et plus largement le même appareil, producteur ou appréciateur: les joues, le palais, les fosses nasales, dont B.S. [Brillat-Savarin] rappelle le rôle gustatif et qui font le beau chant? Manger, parler, chanter (faut-il ajouter: embrasser?) sont des opérations qui ont pour origine le même lieu du corps: la langue coupée, et plus de goût ni de parole. (17)

15. In his *Dictionnaire universel,* Furetière defines *godiveau:* "Espèce de pâté qui se fait de veau haché et d'andouillettes, avec plusieurs ingredients et ragoûts, comme asperges, culs d'artichauts, palais de bœuf, jaune d'œufs, champignons, etc." His last sentence is significant: "Les pâtez de godiveau sont des dejeunez d'ecoliers."

16. A square table does not necessarily imply one where no *préséance* can be observed (*haut bout* as opposed to *bas bout*). At this time tables were often square, with the dishes ranked by size and arranged symmetrically around the table. See Wheaton (138–41) for a detailed description of the *service à la française.* Wheaton also reports that refined manners dictated that the "diner sat up straight, keeping his or her elbows off the table, and generally refrained from impinging on the other guests" (141).

17. Butter and various oils began to tone down the intensity of lemon, vinegar, and verjuice (La Varenne 22–23).

18. The possible pun *rost/rot,* although not in the best of taste (how appropriate!), should not escape the reader, just as the pun *la fumée / le fumet* in v. 196 and the near pun *fumeux/fumier* in v. 73 also convey the speaker's revulsion. It should also be noted that the rabbits served, "animaux domestiques" (v. 90), are described in Furetière as ". . . mangeurs de choux. Ils sont rarement de bon goût." On the other hand, "lapins de garenne" (v. 111) were particularly prized, and most often associated with the landholdings and attendant elaborate facilities belonging to a *grand seigneur,* which, of course, the host certainly is not.

19. Schulz-Buschhaus views the *rost* as a metaphor for the excess, incoherence, and bad taste of baroque literature in particular: "Sie lässt sich nämlich in der Tat—im Zentrum des eigentlichen 'Repas' placiert—als kulinarische Allegorie für das 'extravagante' oder mit einem neueren Begriff: 'barocke' Kunstwerk lesen" (90; "Indeed, it can be read—placed as it is in the middle of the actual meal—as a culinary metaphor for the 'extravagant,' or to use a more modern concept, 'baroque'" [my translation]).

20. La Varenne 14–17. See also Jean-Louis Flandrin's excellent article on evolving gustatory and aesthetic taste, "Pour une histoire du goût." For one seventeenth-century connoisseur's views on proper cuisine, which echo those of the speaker, see Hope 10–36.

21. Qtd. in Flandrin 49.

22. Wheaton describes the elaborate preparation of a *jambon de Mayence:* ". . . the ham is rubbed with salt flavored with pepper, cloves, and anise and then smoked. To prepare it for the table the ham is soaked and boiled, then the rind is peeled back and the meat strewn with parsley and pepper and stuck with cloves. The rind is then returned to its original position and the ham kept in a cold place. It is served with a garnish of flowers" (119).

23. Voltaire elucidates this notion in his article "Goût" in the *Dictionnaire philosophique:*

> Comme le mauvais goût, au physique, consiste à n'être flatté que par des assaisonnements trop piquants et trop recherchés, ainsi le mauvais goût dans les arts est de ne se plaire qu'aux ornements étudiés, et de ne pas sentir la belle nature.

24. R. Bray, *La Formation de la doctrine classique en France* 137–40.

25. See Wood, *Literary Satire and Theory* 42–43, for observations on the threat of silence and the satirist's triumph over it.

26. Brody, *Boileau and Longinus* 85–87, for insights into Boileau's recurring use of images of sight and blindness in his ongoing polemic.

Chapter Four
Reason, Nobility, and the Pursuit of Happiness

1. Brody has shown that *raison* is closely affiliated with the concept of *goût* in his *Boileau and Longinus* 79–81. Claude Chantalat, in his *A la recherche du goût classique* 37–45, devotes a chapter to these associated concepts. See also Pocock 43.

2. Mornet, *Boileau* 17–18; Pocock 43.

3. Ascoli 73 and Escal, in her ed. of Boileau, *Œuvres complètes* 890.

4. In this milieu Jacques Vallée des Barreaux, who lived until 1673 and is now probably best known as a close friend of Théophile de Viau, stands out as a prominent freethinker who denounced reason as the primary origin of man's sufferings. Three verses from a Des Barreaux sonnet summarize this view:

> Je renonce au bon sens, je hay l'intelligence.
> D'autant plus que l'esprit s'élève en connoissance,
> Mieux voit-il le sujet de son affliction.
> (Qtd. in Adam, *Les Libertins au XVII*[e] *siècle* 195)

See Adam, *Les Libertins au XVII*[e] *siècle* 18, 193–97. Boileau's contacts with the *libertin* circle, especially in his early career, have been documented. See, for example, Tallemant des Réaux 2: 30–32.

5. Erasmus 26–27, 30.

6. All of the themes concerning folly and contentment are treated in Erasmus: Man's happiness lies not in how things are but rather in opinions. The so-called wiseman sows only confusion and discord among mortals: "Bring a wiseman to a party: he will disrupt it either by his gloomy silence or his tedious cavils . . . Such a stance could not but earn him the hatred of the people, simply because of this marked difference in mental outlook and style of life. Is anything at all done among mortals that is not full of folly? Isn't everything done by fools, among fools? But if some one person wants to swim against the stream, my advice to him is to imitate Timon by going away to some deserted spot where he can enjoy his wisdom all by himself" (39). Timon brings to mind *Satire I*'s Damon.

7. See Leonard Feinberg's *The Satirist, His Temperament, Motivation, and Influence.*

8. The parade-of-fools motif is perhaps best represented in the well-known 1494 satirical work of the German writer Sebastian Brant, *Ship of Fools.* See especially Joël Lefebvre, *Les Fols et la folie: Étude sur le genre du comique et la création littéraire en Allemagne pendant la Renaissance* 77–169.

9. One is reminded of the foppish Clitandre in Molière's *Le Misanthrope* as described to Célimène by his rival Alceste:

> Vous êtes-vous rendue, avec tout le beau monde,
> Au mérite éclatant de sa perruque blonde?
> (2.1)

Ironically, the well-worn expression is applied to the speaker in Boileau's *Epistre X,* although the intent is quite different:

> Mais aujourd'hui qu'enfin la Vieillesse venuë,
> Sous mes faux cheveux blonds déja toute chénuë.
> (vv. 25–26)

The blond wig could also be a positive token of youthful vigor, as in Régnier's *Satire I, au roi,* when the speaker describes Apollo:

> Phœbus, roy des chansons et des Muses le pere,
> Au plus haut de l'autel se voit un laurier sainct
> Qui sa perruque blonde en guirlandes etraint.
> (vv. 68–70)

10. A near-pun on *manières/manies,* a key word used explicitly in v. 105 in this *Satire,* and which takes on greater resonances in *Satire VII* especially, suggests itself here.

11. Wood, "Boileau, l'équivoque, et l'œuvre ouverte," comments on Boileau's notion that man must have a guide to save him from the dangers of ambiguity: "Dans la poésie, comme dans la vie, il faut sortir du dédale de l'équivoque, de la polysémie et trouver le bon chemin, le seul chemin, l'univoque qui mène à travers le champ sémantique pour arriver à l'intention, au sens, à la raison" (278–79).

12. As in the case of the "perruque blonde," *Le Misanthrope* comes to mind, as Célimène advises Arsinoé:

> Qu'on doit se regarder soi-même un fort longtemps
> Avant que de songer à condamner les gens;
> Qu'il faut mettre le poids d'une vie exemplaire
> Dans les corrections aux autres on veut faire.
>
> (3.3)

13. In Erasmus's *Praise of Folly,* Queen Folly distinguishes between two kinds of madness. The first, which she identifies with the Furies, is akin to that of Boileau's Gambler, who suffers from an unquenchable thirst for winning money. The second affects Chapelain and the deluded Bigot: "It occurs whenever a certain pleasant mental distraction relieves the heart from its anxieties and cares and at the same time soothes it with the balm of manifold pleasures" (58).

14. Here Boileau borrowed a passage from Horace, *Epistles* II.2.128–40, who depicts a similarly deluded but happy fool who is cured of his delusion of enjoying plays in an empty theater. A man of honesty, good judgment, and kindness outside of the theater, he rails against those who rescue him from his "insanity": "'pol, me occidistis, amici / non servastis,' ait, 'cui sic extorta voluptas / et demptus per vim mentis gratissimus error'" (vv. 138–40; "What you have done is to murder me! You have destroyed my delight and / Forcibly swept from my mind the most gloriously sweet of illusions!" [*Complete Works,* trans. Passage]). Immediately before this section Horace, like Boileau, also alludes to the self-beguiled poet: "Praetulerim scriptor delirus inersque videri, / dum mea delectent mala me vel denique fallant, / quam sapere et ringi" (vv. 126–28; "I would much rather be one of those crazy, self-satisfied writers / Charmed by my sorry productions and happy to have them delude me / Than to see clearly and suffer" [*Complete Works,* trans. Passage]). One is reminded of Proverbs 23.9: "Speak not in the ears of a fool: for he will despise the wisdom of thy words."

15. In his *Satire VI* Régnier says much the same thing about honor:

> Ha! que ne suis-je Roy pour cent ou six vingts ans!
> Par un edit public qui fust irrevocable,
> Je bannirois l'Honneur, ce monstre abominable,
> Qui nous trouble l'esprit et nous charme si bien
> Que sans luy les humains icy ne voyent rien,
> Qui trahit la nature, et qui rend imparfaite

Toute chose qu'au goust les delices ont faicte.
(vv. 60–66)

16. See Kaiser, *Praisers of Folly* 53 ff.

17. The speaker takes on this role for Louis XIV at the conclusion of the *Discours au Roy* when he "jumps ship" and abandons his "sinking" poem. See also *Epistre V*, vv. 35–39.

18. In this poem Boileau accepts the conventional but superficial division between *noble* and *roturier*, outlined in 1582 by the jurist Jean Bacquet in his *Traicté . . . concernant les francs-fiefs:*

> En France il y a deux sortes de personnes: les uns sont Nobles, les autres sont Roturiers ou non nobles. Et sous ces deux especes sont comprins tous les habitans du Royaume: soit gens de justice, gens faisans profession des armes . . . & autres, . . . de quelque estat, qualité & condition qu'ils soient. (Qtd. in Huppert 184–85)

19. See Adam, *Les Premières Satires de Boileau* 94–95.

20. "Dans la poésie du XVIIe siècle, le mot 'dieu' désigne souvent un roi, et le mot 'demi-dieu' un prince du sang" (Escal, in her ed. of Boileau, *Œuvres complètes* 902).

21. The fraudulent noble's "mollesse" anticipates the god Mollesse in *Le Lutrin,* Chant II, who laments the vigor of Louis XIV, modern example for the aristocracy:

Helas! qu'est devenu le temps, cet heureux temps,
Où les Rois s'honnoroient du nom de Faineans,
S'endormoient sur le Trône, et me servant sans honte,
Laissoient leur sceptre aux mains ou d'un Maire ou d'un
Comte?
(Ed. Boudhors, vol. 2, vv. 123–26)

The *Discours au Roy* also celebrated Louis's autonomy:

Et qui seul, sans Minstre, à l'exemple des Dieux,
Soûtiens tout par Toi-mesme, et vois tout par Tes yeux.
(vv. 3–4)

22. In this context one should distinguish between *la belle* and *la pure* nature. Seen as the aesthetic reformulation of the latter, *la belle nature* encompasses the values of art and civilization. The racehorse would therefore be a product of *la belle nature.* Being wild, disorderly, and savage, pure nature is inferior to that nature represented by the racehorse. Boileau of course was well aware of this dichotomy, as indicated in his famous dictate in *L'Art poétique* (III.1–4):

Il n'est point de Serpent, ni de Monstre odieux,
Qui, par l'art imité, ne puisse plaire aux yeux.

D'un pinceau delicat l'artifice agreable
Du plus affreux objet fait un objet aimable.
(Ed. Boudhors, vol. 2)

See Saisselin 122–31.

23. In his *Premières Satires de Boileau,* Adam (97) views this portion of the poem as deriving from *libertin* political thought in La Motte and Fontenelle, among others, concerning the myth of the Golden Age ("Aurea prima sata est aetas . . ." [Ovid, *Metamorphoses* I.89 ff.]). Inspired by classical tradition (Hesiod, *Works and Days,* vv. 109–26; Virgil, *Georgics* I.126 ff.; Juvenal, *Satire VI,* vv. 1–24), Boileau expounds further on the theme in *Satire XI;* Damon in *Satire I* also indulges in the comforting fantasy of the *bon vieux temps.* Régnier in his *Satire VI* lamented the ruin of man's primitive innocence:

Je pense, quant à moy, que cest homme fut yvre,
Qui changea le premier l'usage de son vivre
Et rangeant soubs des loys les hommes escartez,
Bastit premierement et villes et citez.
(vv. 97–100)

Perhaps the best-known contemporary manifestation of the myth is the fabulous La Bétique in Fénelon's *Télémaque.* For a discussion of the theme in La Bruyère, see Philip R. Berk, "*De la ville xxii:* La Bruyère and the Golden Age."

24. "Quant aux 'armes'—ou armoiries—, elles ne présentent plus sous l'Ancien Régime que l'intérêt d'une devinette. N'importe qui pouvait se décerner des armoiries, et même les faire enregistrer, contre espèces sonnantes, dans une officine royale qui développa une activité considérable à partir de 1696. Dès lors, et même un peu avant, l'héraldique n'enregistre plus que des vanités" (Goubert 147).

25. On the public "fabrication" of Louis XIV as symbol of the state, see, for example, Peter Burke, *The Fabrication of Louis XIV.*

26. Goubert specifies that the nobility in the Ancien Régime had essentially two broad responsibilities: first, to serve the King either militarily or in the administration of the kingdom; second, to preserve nobility's hereditary prerogatives through procreation within legitimate marriage and, if at all possible, to enhance one's nobility through distinguished deeds in the service of the crown (157–58).

Chapter Five
Looking for Lodging

1. A previous article of mine, "Paris as Barrier: Boileau's *Satire VI,*" *Papers on Seventeenth Century French Literature* 9 (1982): 627–39, furnished ideas and phrasing for the portion of this chapter dealing with *Satire VI.* It is used here with permission.

2. See M. C. Randolphe, "The Structural Design of the Formal Verse Satire."

3. It should be noted that Horace also played a significant role in the formulation of *l'embarras de Paris.* In *Epistles* II.2.65–86, Horace's speaker curses urban life as an impediment to his creativity and enumerates the city's numerous "blockages":

> festinat calidus mulis gerulisque redemptor,
> torquet nunc lapidem, nunc ingens machina tignum,
> tristia robustis luctantur funera plaustris,
> hac rabiosa fugit canis, hac lutulenta ruit sus:
> i nunc et versus tecum meditare canoros.
> scriptorum chorus omnis amat nemus et fugit urbem.
>
> (Just a builder with mules and porters in a furious rush,
> a giant crane lifting now a beam and now a boulder,
> howling funeral trains tangled up with heavy wagons,
> a mad dog running here, and there a speedy, slimy sow.
> You try it, take a walk and make up pretty verses!
> The whole poetic chorus loves the groves and flees the city.
> [*Satires and Epistles,* trans. Fuchs, vv. 72–77])

4. For a meticulous analysis of "Le Mauvais Logement," see David Lee Rubin, "Consciousness and the External World in a Caprice by Saint-Amant."

5. The night-day analogy evident in the poem further recalls Saint-Amant's "Le Mauvais Logement," in which explicit nocturnal attacks coincide with implicit daytime military maneuvers.

6. Smith 122–24.

7. Cf. Juvenal, *Satire III,* vv. 302–04:

> Nec tamen hoc tantum metuas: nam qui spoliette
> Non deerit: clausis domibus, postquam omnis ubique
> Fixa catenatae siluit compago tabernae.
>
> (Nor is this alone what you have to fear; for a Thief may
> rob you when the House is close barr'd, and the Shutters
> of all Shops are pinn'd, and the Doors chain'd.
> [*The Satires of Juvenal Translated*])

8. Conversely, the speaker in the *Epistre VI* luxuriates in the idyllic peace of the countryside that allows him to pursue his *rêveries:*

> Tantost, un livre en main, errant dans les préries
> J'occupe ma raison d'utiles rêveries.
> Tantost cherchant la fin d'un vers que je construy
> Je trouve au coin d'un bois le mot qui m'avoit fuy.
> (vv. 25–28)

We are also reminded of Boileau's remark in his *Discours de l'auteur pour servir d'apologie à la Satire XII sur l'équivoque:* "Je me promenois dans mon jardin à Auteuil, et rêvois en marchant à un Poëme que je voulois faire contre les mauvais Critiques de notre siècle" (*Œuvres complètes,* ed. Escal 88).

9. Brody, "Boileau et la critique poétique" 233–34.

10. Borgerhoff, "Boileau Satirist *Anima Gratia*" 254.

11. Alternatively, Wood examines Boileau's *Satire VII* in light of Horace, *Satires* I.4. See his *Literary Satire and Theory* 38–47.

12. Although not as obvious a source as Horace, Juvenal's *Satire I,* from which comes the dictum "difficile est satiram non scribere" (" 'tis hard to hold from Writing [Satire]" [v. 30]), discusses the genre of satire especially in its framing sections (vv. 1–31, 150–71). Persius's program poem *Satire I* contains many of the same themes: self-justification for his generic choice, condemnation of contemporary literary standards, appeal to prior examples, etc.

13. In the opening lines of Régnier's *Satire XV,* the speaker also laments his servitude under an omnipotent Muse:

> Ouy j'escry rarement et me plais de le faire,
> Non pas que la paresse en moy soit ordinaire,
> Mais si tost que je prens la plume à ce dessein,
> Je croy prendre en galere une rame en la main:
> Je sens, au second vers, que la Muse me dicte,
> Et contre sa fureur ma raison se despite.
>
> (vv. 1–6)

And later:

> Comme on voit par exemple en ces vers où j'accuse
> Librement le caprice où me porte la Muse,
> Qui me repaist de baye en ses fous passe-temps
> Et malgré moy me fait aux vers perdre le temps.
>
> (vv. 101–04)

14. Pocock (29) points out the antitheses in the poem's opening lines, which in turn complement his notion that the speaker "remains divided against himself" in *Satire VII.*

15. The standard historical explanation for this reference to eulogies focuses on Boileau's chagrin over Chapelain's substantial financial compensation for a bombastic sonnet in praise of Louis XIV. See Adam, *Les Premières Satires de Boileau* 28–29. In fact, prior satirical program poems (and Boileau's own poems) have sarcastically suggested soothing encomia as alternatives to mordant denunciation. See, for example, Persius, *Satire I,* vv. 110–11: "per me equidem sint omnia protinus alba; / nil moror. euge omnes, omnes bene, mirae eritis res" ("The whole lot's fine forthwith for all I care, no matter! / 'Bravo!' to everyone and, everyone, 'Hooray!' You'll be my / Ideal" [19–21]).

16. "One of the recurring themes of the satire is that satire writes itself . . ." (Wood, *Literary Satire and Theory* 45).

17. Much discussion has centered on the people behind the names in vv. 44–45. Typically, Boileau changed the names over the successive editions of the *Satires.* See, for example, Ascoli 99–101; Boudhors, in his ed. of Boileau, *Œuvres complètes* 1: 251–52; and Adam, *Les Premières Satires de Boileau* 35–44.

18. "Les adversaires de Boileau faisaient leur cette image. Chapelain, dans son *Discours satirique,* le traitait de 'chien enragé'" (Ascoli 101). Boileau's satiric predecessors exploited the same metaphor: see Lucilius, fragment 1000–01: "Inde canino ricto oculisque involem" ("Then let me fly at him with a dog's grin and glare"); Horace, *Satires* II.1.84–85: "si quis / opprobriis dignum latraverit, integer ipsi?" ("What if, though I've barked at those worth barking at, I'm guiltless?" [*Satires and Epistles,* trans. Fuchs]); Persius, *Satire I,* vv. 107–10: "sed quid opus teneras mordaci radere vero / auriculas? vide sis ne maiorum tibi forte / limina frigescant: sonat hic de nara canina / littera" ("Must you, though, scrub delicate ears with truths / that bite? Take care the doorways of the Great don't maybe cool towards you. There are noises here of curled lips and the Letters dogs can say").

19. From Horace, *Satires* I.4.39–42:

> primum ego me illorum, dederim quibus esse poetas,
> excerpam numero: neque enim concludere versum
> dixeris esse satis; neque si qui scribat uti nos
> sermoni proporia, putes hunc esse poetam.
>
> (In the first place, I don't count myself among those
> I consider poets; it's a mistake to think that putting words
> in meter is the only thing they do, or that anyone
> like me—my things are more like conversations—is a poet.
> [*Satires and Epistles,* trans. Fuchs])

20. Brody, "Boileau et la critique poétique" 241.

21. Horace's speaker is determined to pursue his calling (*Satires* II.1):

> ne longum faciam: seu me tranquilla senectus
> exspectat seu mors atris circumvolat alis,
> dives, inops, Romae, seu fors ita iusserit, exsul,
> quisquis erit vitae scribam color.
>
> (Here's my point. Whether peaceful aging lies ahead
> or death now hovers over me, circling on black wings,
> wealthy or poor, in Rome or, as fate will it, in exile,
> whatever my life's color, I'll write.
> [*Satires and Epistles,* trans. Fuchs, vv. 57–60])

22. Boileau is following a long tradition among the satirists in question. Horace mentions Lucilius in his *Satires* I.4.6–13 and 10.1–5, and refers specifically to him as the inventor of satire in II.1.63–64. A century later in his *Satire I,* Juvenal chooses to follow the examples of the trailblazer Lucilius (vv. 19–20) and his successor Horace (v. 51). It is interesting to note that in Horace, *Satires* I.4.105–28, the speaker claims that his "father" formed his character by citing specific individuals as examples to be emulated or to be shunned.

23. Boileau's use of "bons mots" in this context reverses Horace's *mala . . . carmina* ("bad poems") mentioned by Trebatius in *Satires* II.1.82. While Trebatius refers to the legal restriction against evil incantations, the speaker immediately assumes that the expression denotes aesthetically bad verse. His rejoinder concerning *bona* [*carmina*] (v. 83) appears to correspond to the moral and aesthetic implications of Boileau's "bons mots":

> "si mala condiderit in quem quis carmina, ius est iudiciumque."
> Esto, si quis mala; sed bona si quis
> iudice condiderit laudatus Caesare?
>
> (if one party composes bad poems about another, we have
> a procedure and a penalty. *Hor:* Yes, if they're bad,
> but what if they're good and praised by Caesar?
> [*Satires and Epistres,* trans. Fuchs, vv. 82–84])

24. Contrary to the speaker's assertion, it appears that Juvenal, although living a long life of some eighty years, did indeed die in unfortunate circumstances. Juvenal himself warns of satire's dangers in his *Satire I,* vv. 147–57. Most accounts agree that he died in misery after being exiled for a satire lampooning corruption in the court of the emperor Domitian. See Highet, *Juvenal the Satirist* 26–31. It is likely, however, that the "tragique fin" referred to here has a figurative connotation.

25. This is indeed the case with Boileau himself. See Mornet, *Boileau* 15 ff. Only in 1666, after the unauthorized "édition monstrueuse" of Rouen, was Boileau obliged to publish the first approved edition of *Satires I* through *VII* and the *Discours au Roy.* Public readings and circulating manuscripts assured the poet's notoriety well before 1666.

26. Juvenal in his *Satire I* reverses this situation, deploring the awful works that authors force the speaker to hear. The opening line encapsulates his lament: "Semper ego auditor tantum? nunquamne reponam" ("Must I forever hear? and ne'er reply?").

27. Conversely, despite his self-righteous indignation against foreigners, homosexuals, and false patrons, Juvenal's speaker in his *Satire I* retreats from his strong stance (he will attack only the dead! [vv. 170–71]) when the interlocutor warns him of the dangers of satire.

28. Boileau's notable predecessors—Horace, Juvenal, Persius, Régnier—all invoked their generic forefathers.

29. Despite this philosophical focus, it is difficult, however, to accept Adam's contention that in *Satire VIII* "le satirique abandonne la satire" (*Les Premières Satires de Boileau* 225).

30. The Italian philosopher Lucilio Vanini appears to have influenced Théophile's thinking:

> Le livre de Vanini en 1616 n'était-il pas intitulé: *De admirandus Naturae, reginae deaeque mortalium, arcanius?* Reine et déesse de l'univers, oui, telle est Nature, au sens qu'après ses maîtres, Théophile donne à ce mot. (Adam, *Théophile de Viau et la libre pensé française en 1620* 207)

See also Adam, *Les Premières Satires de Boileau* 226–27.

31. Théophile de Viau, *Œuvres poétiques,* ed. Streicher 1: 89.

32. One thinks of Montaigne's *Apologie de Raymond Sebon:*

> La plus calamiteuse et fraile de toutes les creatures, c'est l'homme, et quant et quant la plus orgueilleuse. Elle se sent et se void logée icy, parmi la bourbe et le fient du monde, attachée et clouée à la pire, plus morte et croupie partie de l'univers, au dernier estage du logis et le plus esloigné de la voute celeste, avec les animaux de la pire condition des trois. (452)

Montaigne's appraisal of what he sees as reason in the animal world places man in a median position between the exalted master of the universe and the most wretched of God's creatures.

33. "Go to the ant, thou sluggard; consider her ways, and be wise" (Proverbs 6.6).

34. It hardly need be said that satire has traditionally been viewed as a minor genre, far below epic, tragedy, or even comedy.

35. Perhaps the best example of this is Erasmus, whose speaker in *The Praise of Folly* (first published in 1511) is Folly herself, who turns out—naturally—to be a gifted sophist. See xx–xxi.

36. "Au Palais . . . on désigne sous le nom de doyen le magistrat le plus ancien de chaque catégorie; et parmi les magistrats, tous solennels, ceux-là affectent plus de solennité encore" (Ascoli 106).

37. Cf. Horace, *Satires* I.1.32–38:

> . . . sicut
> parvola, nam exemplo est, magni formica laboris
> ore trahit quodcumque potest atque addit acervo
> quem struit, haud ignara ac non incauta futuri.
> quae, simul inversum contristat Aquarius annum,
> non usquam prorepit et illis utitur ante
> quaesitis sapiens.

> (. . . Look at
> the tiny ant [they'll tell you] who works hard and drags in
> by mouth all that goes into the store she gathers;
> she thinks about the future and prepares for it.
> But as soon as January shades the cycling year,

> the ant stops crawling out and enjoys whatever she has.
> She has good sense.
>
> [*Satires and Epistles,* trans. Fuchs])

38. Rabelais's Bridoye in *Le Tiers Livre* offers a notable example.

39. "Il s'agissait, d'après Brossette, 'd'un petit livre, relié proprement en manière d'Heures, où au lieu des images que l'on met dans les livres de prières, (Bussy avait inséré) les portraits en miniature de quelques hommes de la cour dont les femmes étaient soupçonnées de galanteries'" (qtd. in Ascoli 107–08).

40. In his *Satires* I.1.32 ff., Horace juxtaposes the ant and the miser, making this analogy much more explicit.

41. Ascoli's note (111) asserts that these lines on *l'homme policé* "sont assez lourds, et Brossette et Le Verrier s'accordent à dire qu'ils lui ont coûté beaucoup de peine."

42. A probable allusion to the court case of the Marquis de Langey, begun in 1657. See Escal, in her ed. of Boileau's *Œuvres complétes* 916; Boudhors, in his ed. of Boileau's *Œuvres complétes* 1: 260.

43. The father's mathematics lesson and naked cynicism in vv. 181–210 recall Horace's lament in the *Ars poetica,* vv. 323–32, over the purely computational, mercantile education drilled into Roman children, training that forever destroys the soul's capacity for poetry. See also *Satires* II.3.94–98. It also anticipates Lui's attitudes and instructional techniques for his son in Diderot's *Le Neveu de Rameau.*

44. One is reminded of the writer who composes "un éloge ennuyeux, un froid panegyrique" solely for money in the preceding *Satire VII,* v. 9.

45. Best known for his *Critique désintéressée sur les satires du temps,* in which he called Boileau "un censeur triste et sévère," Cotin has also been credited with *Despréaux ou la Satire des satires* (1666; "Je dis mon sentiment, je ne suis point menteur, / J'appelle Horace Horace, et Boileau traducteur") and the *Discours satirique au cynique Despréaux* (1667?; "C'est porter la satire au-delà de ses justes limites que de l'employer contre les mauvaises Poésies si l'on n'entend par ce mot celles qui, comme la vôtre, s'en prennent à la Religion et à l'Etat, ou qui par une doctrine scandaleuse et impure comme la vôtre tendent à la dépravation des mœurs" [see Beugnot and Zubner 10–11, 113–16]).

46. Cf. Régnier, *Satire IX,* vv. 249–52:

> Mais, Rapin, à leur goust si les vieux sont profanes
> Si Virgille, le Tasse et Ronsard sont des asnes,
> Sans perdre en ces discours le tans que nous perdons,
> Allons comme eux aux champs et mangeons des chardons.

47. Ovid, *Metamorphoses* XI.84–193, recounts the legend of King Midas of Phrygia. Apollo gave him the ears of an ass after Midas, alone among all the listeners, stated his preference for Pan's rustic pipes over Apollo's lyre.

48. Fabulists have exploited animal characters for this purpose for many centuries. The traditional figure of the "wise" fool, and Erasmus's use of Queen Folly as the spokesperson in *The Praise of Folly,* are variations of this device. This is also reminiscent of the medieval Feast of Fools, in which the fool's costume included a cap with ass's ears. See the introduction of Clarence H. Miller's translation of *The Praise of Folly.*

49. Le Verrier states in his *Commentaire* that the poem was addressed to Claude Morel, an eminent professor "qu'on appeloit en Sorbonne Machoire d'Asne parce que son menton avoit en effet quelque rapport avec la mâchoire d'âne" (qtd. in Escal, in her ed. of Boileau's *Œuvres complètes* 912). This partial explanation for the donkey's speech at the close of *Satire VIII* seems forced at best. Boudhors offers additional clarifications (in his ed. of Boileau's *Œuvres complètes* 255–56).

50. In this regard we may refer to La Fontaine's "Le Vieillard et l'âne," in which the wise donkey condemns all masters, whether he be the old man or the Devil himself:

> —Et que m'importe donc, dit l'Ane, à qui je sois?
> Sauvez-vous, et me laissez paître:
> Notre ennemi, c'est notre Maître:
> Je vous le dis en bon François.
>
> (160)

Chapter Six
Withdrawal

1. In his crucial article, Borgerhoff saw the intertextual significance of *Satire IX,* without, however, further exploring the idea: "Thus the whole poem has to be read in the light of the previous *Satires,* indeed in the light of Boileau's whole career in the literary world up to this time" ("Boileau Satirist *Animi Gratia*" 246).

2. Brody's definition of Boileau's use of the word *esprit* in his translation of Longinus is useful here:

> By *esprit* Boileau seems to mean here, as often in the body of his works, not merely an innate potential, but an effective creative power, having as much to do with judgment as with gift. . . . deep within the creative mind he saw a complex connivance of the natural and the intellectual, vitality and restraint. (*Boileau and Longinus* 59)

3. Raison's self-importance inevitably suggests analogies to certain of Molière's characters, among whom are Mme Pernelle's tone and manner as she rebukes each member of the family at the beginning of *Tartuffe,* and Arsinoé in *Le Misanthrope.* Pocock has emphasized the dramatic structure of *Satire IX:* "Indeed, the poem begins and ends like a play" (55).

4. Borgerhoff: "With this reference to one of his favorite butts, the abbé de Pure, Boileau-censor who, we understand is at least partly a make-believe Boileau, lifts the mask and shows himself to be really Boileau himself, as we know him after all" ("Boileau Satirist *Animi Gratia*" 247).

5. An added fillip to Raison's succinct gibes at Gautier and de Pure is the tone of utter confidence with which he castigates Esprit. Given his own sense of righteousness, his insults, unlike the "libres caprices" of Esprit, must be accepted as irrefutable facts, since they do *not* originate in the latter's "foible" and "stérile" (v. 15) mind! Gautier is an abrasive, annoying presence in the courtroom and de Pure a terrible poet, and that's all there is to it!

6. See *Discours,* vv. 17 ff. and *Satire I,* vv. 89–95.

7. The minor poet Fléchier had just published the elegy "La Reyne au Roy sur les travaux de la Guerre," which celebrates the recent capture of Lille by the King's troops. See Escal, in her ed. of Boileau's *Œuvres complètes* 920.

8. Cotin's *Critique désintéressé sur les satires du temps* (1666) and *Discours satirique au cynique Despréaux* (1667) may have occasioned *Satire IX.* After the publication of the *Satires* in 1666:

> Cotin surtout s'agite. Dans les salons qu'il fréquente, il se répand en propos contre le satirique. Il dénonce en lui un esprit dangereux. Dans l'écrivain qui a bafoué la raison, dans l'homme qui a raillé toutes les puissances, il découvre un péril pour la foi et pour l'ordre social. (Adam, *Les Premières Satires de Boileau* 192)

9. The word played a key role in *Satire V* on the moral and spiritual nullity of the false noble, who "Se pare insolemment du merite d'autrui" (v. 7), a charge that Raison will soon direct at Esprit.

10. As with any praise from the satirist's pen, irony and ambiguity remain open possibilities here. The juxtaposition of Voiture and Horace, however, appears to minimize this likelihood. See Wood, "Boileau, l'équivoque, et l'œuvre ouverte."

11. *Boileau and Longinus* 63.

12. Note the judicial vocabulary applied to each example:

> Tous les jours à la Cour un Sot de qualité
> Peut juger de travers avec impunité.
>
> (vv. 173–74)

> Un Clerc, pour quinze sous, sans craindre le hola,
> Peut aller au Parterre attaquer Attila.
>
> (vv. 177–78)

> Il n'est Valet d'Auteur, ni Copiste à Paris,
> Qui la balance en main ne péze les écrits.
>
> (vv. 181–82)

Un Auteur à genoux, dans une humble Préface,
Au Lecteur qu'il ennuye, a beau demander grace;
Il ne gagnera rien sur ce Juge irrité,
Qui lui fait son procés de pleine autorité.
(vv. 187–90)

13. In his *Satire I,* vv. 119–21, Persius also alludes to the story of Midas, drawing an explicit analogy between the satirist and the barber. In the same passage Persius also refers to his artistic forebears Lucilius and Horace, a device that Boileau mimics with the important theme of example/model fundamental to this section.

14. See Régnier, *Satires IV, X,* and *XV.*

15. "Lélie" refers to Lucilius's high-born friend and protector Caius Laelius. Verse 275 alludes in all likelihood to Horace, *Satires* II.1.71–78, in which the speaker emphasizes the protection afforded the impertinent Lucilius by such high-placed friends as Laelius and Scipio.

16. See Horace, *Satires* I.10.3–4: "Yet this same satirist, because he scoured the city / with large quantities of salt, was praised on the same page" (*Satires and Epistles,* trans. Fuchs). Boileau also uses the metaphor in *Epistre X,* in which the speaker addresses his verse, which:

Et par le prompt effet d'un sel réjoüissant
Devenir quelquefois proverbes en naissant.
(vv. 11–12)

In the preface to the 1701 edition of the *Œuvres diverses* Boileau employs the metaphor to define an essential element in poetry that stands the test of time: "Un ouvrage a beau estre approuvé d'un petit nombre de Connoisseurs, s'il n'est plein d'un certain agrément et d'un certain sel propre à piquer le goust general des Hommes . . ." (*Œuvres complètes,* ed. Escal 1).

17. See Wood, "Boileau, l'équivoque, et l'œuvre ouverte" 281–82.

18. For example: *IX,* v. 287, "Puisque vous le voulez, je vais changer de stile": *VII,* v. 1, "Muse, changeons de stile, et quittons la Satire"; *IX,* v. 288, "Je le declare donc. Quinaut est un Virgile": *II,* v. 20, "La raison dit Virgile, et la rime Quinaut"; *IX,* vv. 289–90, "Pradon comme un Soleil en nos ans a paru. / Pelletier écrit mieux qu'Ablancourt ni Patru": *VII,* vv. 44–45, "Je rencontre à la fois Perrin et Pelletier, / Bonnecourse, Pradon, Colletet, Titreville"; *IX,* vv. 291–92, "Cotin à ses Sermons traînant toute la terre, / Fend les flots d'Auditeurs pour aller à sa chaire": *III,* vv. 59–60, "Si l'on n'est plus au large assis en un festin, / Qu'aux sermons de Cassaigne, ou de l'Abbé Cotin."

19. One is reminded of the prince's "penetrating" wisdom in *Tartuffe:*

Nous vivons sous un prince ennemi de la fraude,
Un prince dont les yeux se font jour dans les cœurs,
Et que ne peut tromper tout l'art des imposteurs.

> D'un fin discernement sa grande âme pourvue
> Sur les choses toujours jette une droite vue.
>
> (vv. 1906–10)

20. *Satire X,* which according to Le Verrier was composed over a period of twenty years, first appeared, separately from the other *Satires,* in 1694. It is interesting to note that after the date October 22, 1669, in the "Chronologie de la vie et des œuvres de Boileau" in her edition of the *Œuvres complètes,* Escal writes: "Il a cessé d'être un pilier de cabaret. Il n'écrit plus de satires. Il s'assagit" (xxxv). The phrase "pilier de cabaret" comes directly from Chapelain's libelous *Discours satirique au cynique Despréaux:* "On parle de vous comme d'un fameux pilier de cabaret, d'un fameux joueur de farces, d'un fameux batteur de pavé . . ." (qtd. in R. Bray, *Boileau, l'homme et l'œuvre* 24). Escal's interpretation follows the widely accepted view that the *Satires* form the youthful and vigorous first stage of Boileau's career, followed by the "législateur du Parnasse" period of the 1670s. Commenting on the *Satires,* Nitze and Dargan are typical: "All these faults and foibles of the time are scored by Boileau in dozens of passages. Thereupon, having accomplished the work of destruction, the theorist in Boileau turns to erect the working code of Classicism" (326).

21. Major poetic and critical works published between 1668 and 1694 include:

Epistres I–IX (*I–V,* 1674; *VII–IX,* 1683);
L'Art poétique (1674);
Le Lutrin (Chants I–IV, 1674; V–VI, 1683);
Le Traité du Sublime (1674);
Dialogues des Héros de roman (first published in Holland in 1688, published in France as *Dialogue des Morts* in 1701);
Ode sur la prise de Namur (1693).

22. The change in emphasis from *Satires I–IX* to the *Epistres* has long been a subject of discussion in Boileau scholarship. See, for example, Mornet's chapter "La Componction de Boileau," in his *Boileau* 91–98; R. Bray, "Transition," *Boileau, l'homme et l'œuvre* 44–54; Pocock 58–60. The first two verses of *Epistre I* are instructive:

> Grand Roy, c'est vainement qu'abjurant la Satire,
> Pour Toy seul desormais j'avois fait vœu d'écrire.

23. ". . . the satires of the early 1660s are fun. They show in the highest degree Boileau's *vis comica,* and are hard to read without laughing aloud" (Pocock 39).

24. In his *Nicolas Boileau-Despréaux: révolutionnaire et conformiste* (126–28), Joret insists on the ambivalence of Boileau's attitude toward his métier throughout his career. In the conclusion of the poet's last work, *Satire XII* (completed 1706), the speaker returns to the recurrent idea of retreat from poetry.

Conclusion

1. Borgerhoff, "Boileau Satirist *Animi Gratia*" 254.

2. In his anatomy of rhetoric, Aristotle defines *ethos* as proof deriving from the character of the speaker. The persuasive effect of any satirical discourse depends of course upon the reader's positive assessment of the rhetorician's character. See, for example, Maynard Mack, "The Muse of Satire."

3. See the chapter entitled "L' 'Honnête homme' et la 'politesse,'" in Mornet's *L'Histoire de la littérature française classique, 1660–1700* 97–124.

4. Adam, *Théophile de Viau et la libre pensée française en 1620;* René Pintard, *Le Libertinage érudit en France au XVIIe siècle.*

5. Théophile de Viau, *Œuvres poétiques,* ed. Streicher 1: 88–89.

6. Boileau's hunger for fame in his early career can be seen in a letter to Brossette, dated June 16, 1708. He is referring to *Satire XII,* "Contre l'équivoque":

> Je doute neanmoins que celle que j'ay composée contre ce dernier monstre [l'équivoque] voye le jour avant ma mort par ce que je fuis autant aujourdhui de faire parler de moi que j'en ay esté avide autre fois. (*Œuvres complétes,* ed. Boudhors 6: 114)

7. In the preface to the *Epistres nouvelles* (*X–XII*), published in 1698, Boileau expresses quite another point of view: "Le Public n'est pas un Juge qu'on puisse corrompre, ni qui se regle par les passions d'autruy" (*Œuvres complètes,* ed. Boudhors 2: 138). Brody comments on Boileau's public and his attitudes toward it:

> When Boileau implies that the public of his day was composed of connoisseurs [in his 1701 preface], he is projecting his personal values over the vast, cluttered screen of contemporary taste. He attributes his own standards to those who are to judge him and to his fellow writers. This is perhaps why he published so little and with such misgivings. The *Bolaeana* report that "M. Despréaux n'a jamais rien imprimé qu'à son corps défendant; les jugements du public lui ayant toujours fait peur: c'est un scrupule qu'il a porté jusqu'à sa dernière vieillesse." (*Boileau and Longinus* 105)

8. See Timothy Hampton's introduction to *Baroque Topographies: Literature/History/Philosophy* for a general discussion of the concept of aesthetic site.

9. See especially Pocock 59–69. Fanny Népote-Desmarres maintains that the *Satires* and the *Epistres* diverge little from one another: "De fait, chez Boileau, il y a même parfois plus de parenté entre une satire et une épître qu'entre deux satires . . ." (185). The emphasis on moral purpose and the relative lack of direct and virulent mockery, however, clearly delineate the *Epistres*. The speaker's use of morally charged imperatives to the addressee in the *Epistres* is one signal of this change. For example:

> Joüissons à loisir du fruit de Tes bien-faits,
> Et nous lassons point des douceurs de la Paix.
> (*Epistre I*, vv. 59–60)
>
> Abbé, n'entrepren point mesme un juste procés.
> N'imite point ces Fous dont la sotte avarice
> Va de ses revenus engraisser la Justice.
> (*II*, vv. 24–26)
>
> Non, ne croy pas que Claude habile à se tromper,
> Soit sensible aux traits dont tu le sçais frapper.
> (*III*, vv. 7–8)
>
> Guilleragues, plain-toi de mon humeur legere;
> Si jamais entraîné d'une ardeur étrangere,
> Ou d'un vil interest reconnoissant la loi,
> Je cherche mon bonheur autre part que chez moi.
> (*V*, 145–49)
>
> C'est à toi, Lamoignon, que le rang, la naissance,
> Le merite éclatant, et la haute éloquence
> Appellent dans Paris aux sublimes emplois.
> (*VI*, vv. 129–31)
>
> Cependant laisse ici gronder quelques Censeurs,
> Qu'aigrissent de tes vers les charmantes douceurs.
> (*VII*, vv. 85–86)

10. Wood, "La Poétique de l'épître chez Boileau." Many commentators have noted the epistle's vague generic parameters:

> Ainsi l'épître apparaît-elle comme un genre protéiforme aux virtualités multiples, non seulement métaphorique (élégie, satire, épigramme), mais, bien plus «gigogne», capable d'enchâsser une diatribe satirique, une tirade élogieuse ou un retour sur soi élégiaque. De plus, en ce qui concerne sa vocation à délivrer une information, à établir la communication avec un destinataire, le genre peut s'actualiser en chronique voire en gazette, des faits les plus quotidiens aux événements historiques. (Génetiot 104–05)

11. Lanson repeats the story in which Boileau recites verses from *Epistre I* to an appreciative Louis XIV:

> Le roi depuis longtemps avait marqué du goût pour ses vers, jusqu'à quitter le billard une fois pour les entendre, quand

> Vivonne lui amena le poète, qui récita des morceaux du *Lutrin* et la fin de la *Première Epître* . . . Le roi fut charmé . . . Il loua le poète, lui donna deux mille livres de pension, avec un privilège pour l'impression de ses ouvrages. Cette scène n'a pu se passer avant 1672. (24)

12. In the *Epistre VIII, au Roy,* however, the speaker expresses some—momentary—remorse for having abandoned the *stile* of the early *Satires:*

> Il me semble, GRAND ROY, dans mes nouveaux écrits,
> Que mon encens payé n'est plus du mesme prix.
> J'ay peur que l'Univers, qui sçait ma récompence,
> N'impute mes transports à ma reconnoissance.
> (vv. 75–78)

Works Consulted

Ackerman, Simone. "Les *Satires* de Boileau: Un Théâtre de l'absurde avant la lettre." *Ordre et contestation au temps des classiques: Actes du 21e colloque du Centre Méridional de Rencontres sur le XVIIe siècle jumelé avec le 23e colloque de la North American Society for Seventeenth Century French Literature (Marseille, 19–23 juin 1991).* Ed. R. Duchêne and P. Ronzeaud. 2 vols. Biblio 17 73. Paris, Seattle, and Tübingen: Papers on French Seventeenth Century Literature, 1992. 1: 255–66.

Adam, Antoine. *Les Libertins au XVIIe siècle.* Paris: Buchet/Chastel, 1964.

———. *Les Premières Satires de Boileau (I–IX).* Lille, 1941. Rpt. Genève: Slatkine, 1970.

———. *Théophile de Viau et la libre pensée française en 1620.* Paris, 1935. Rpt. Genève: Slatkine, 1965.

Anderson, William S. "Poetic Arrangement from Vergil to Ovid." *Poems in Their Place: The Intertextuality and Order of Poetic Collections.* Ed. Neil Fraistat. Chapel Hill: U of North Carolina P, 1986. 44–65.

Armstrong, David. *Horace.* New Haven and London: Yale UP, 1989.

Ascoli, Georges. *Boileau, Satires de I à IX.* "Les Cours de Sorbonne." Paris: CDU, 1967.

Aulotte, Robert. *Mathurin Régnier: Les Satires.* Paris: CEDES, 1983.

Baglioli, Mario. "Etiquette, Interdependence, and Sociability in Seventeenth-Century Science." *Critical Inquiry* 22.2 (1996): 193–238.

Bakhtin, Mikhail. *Rabelais and His World.* Trans. H. Iswolsky. Cambridge: MIT, 1968.

Barthes, Roland. "Toward a Psychosociology of Contemporary Food Consumption." *Food and Drink in History.* Ed. Robert Forster and Orest Ranum. Baltimore: Johns Hopkins UP, 1979. 166–73.

Berk, Philip R. "*De la ville xxii:* La Bruyère and the Golden Age." *French Review* 47 (1974): 1072–80.

Beugnot, Bernard, and Roger Zuber. *Boileau: Visages anciens, visages nouveaux, 1665–1970.* Montréal: Les Presses de l'Université de Montréal, 1973.

Bloom, Edward A, and Lillian D. Bloom. *Satire's Persuasive Voice.* Ithaca: Cornell UP, 1979.

Bloom, Harold. *The Anxiety of Influence.* New York: Oxford UP, 1973.

Boileau-Despréaux, Nicolas. *Œuvres complètes.* Ed. Charles-H. Boudhors. 7 vols. 1934–43. Paris: Les Belles Lettres, 1952–60.

Boileau-Despréaux, Nicolas. *Œuvres complètes.* Ed. Françoise Escal. Pléiade. Paris: Gallimard, 1966.

Borgerhoff, E. B. O. "Boileau Satirist *Animi Gratia.*" *Romanic Review* 43 (1952): 241–55.

———. *The Freedom of French Classicism.* Princeton: Princeton UP, 1950.

Braund, Susan H. "City and Country in Roman Satire." Ed. S. H. Braund. *Satire and Society in Ancient Rome.* Exeter: Exeter UP, 1989. 23–47.

———. *Roman Verse Satire.* Oxford: Oxford UP, 1982.

Bray, Bernard. "Dialectique de l'ordre et du désordre dans les *Satires* de Boileau." *Ordre et contestation au temps des classiques: Actes du 21e colloque du Centre Méridional de Rencontres sur le XVIIe siècle jumelé avec le 23e colloque de la North American Society for Seventeenth Century French Literature (Marseille, 19–23 juin 1991).* Ed. R. Duchêne and P. Ronzeaud. 2 vols. Biblio 17 73. Paris, Seattle, and Tübingen: Papers on French Seventeenth Century Literature, 1992. 1: 267–74.

Bray, René. *Boileau, l'homme et l'œuvre.* Paris: Boivin, 1942.

———. *La Formation de la doctrine classique.* Paris: Hachette, 1927.

Brillat-Savarin, Jean Anthelme. *Physiologie du goût.* Ed. Roland Barthes. Paris: Hermann, 1975.

Brody, Jules. *Boileau and Longinus.* Genève: Droz, 1958.

———. "Boileau et la critique poétique." *Critique et création littéraires en France au XVIIe siècle.* Actes du colloque international du CNRS 557. Paris: CNRS, 1977. 231–50.

Brooks, Cleanth. *The Well Wrought Urn.* New York: Harcourt, 1948.

Brown, James W. *Fictional Meals and Their Function in the French Novel.* Toronto: U of Toronto P, 1984.

Burke, Peter. *The Fabrication of Louis XIV.* New Haven and London: Yale UP, 1992.

Chantalat, Claude. *A la recherche du goût classique.* Paris: Klincksieck, 1992.

Clarac, Pierre. *Boileau.* Collection "Les Grands Auteurs Français." Paris: Mellotte, n.d.

Corum, Robert T., Jr. "Paris as Barrier: Boileau's *Satire VI.*" *Papers on French Seventeenth Century Literature* 9 (1982): 627–39.

Cronk, Nicholas. "The Singular Voice: Monologism and French Classical Discourse." *Continuum* 1 (1989): 175–202.

Debailly, Pascal. "Juvénal en France au XVIe et au XVIIe siècle." *La Satire en vers au XVIIe siècle.* Ed. Louise Godard de Donville. Littératures classiques 24. Paris: Klincksieck, 1995. 28–47.

Diderot, Denis. *Le Neveu de Rameau.* Ed. Jean Fabre. Genève: Droz, 1963.

Doirion, Norman. "Le Pauvre Poète: De la censure des mœurs parisiennes à la sublimation esthétique." *Ordre et contestation au temps des classiques: Actes du 21e colloque du Centre Méridional de Rencontres sur le XVIIe siècle jumelé avec le 23e colloque de la North American Society for Seventeenth Century French Literature (Marseille, 19–23 juin 1991).* Ed. R. Duchêne and P. Ronzeaud. 2 vols. Biblio 17 73. Paris, Seattle, and Tübingen: Papers on French Seventeenth Century Literature, 1992. 1: 247–54.

Duval, Edwin. *Poesis and Poetic Tradition.* York, SC: French Literature Publications, 1981.

Edelman, Nathan. "*L'Art poétique:* 'Longtemps plaire et jamais ne lasser.'" *Studies in Seventeenth-Century French Literature Presented to Morris Bishop.* Ed. J.-J. Demorest. Ithaca: Cornell UP, 1962.

Erasmus. *The Praise of Folly.* Trans. Clarence H. Miller. New Haven and London: Yale UP, 1979.

Evans, Lewis, trans. *The Satires of Juvenal, Persius, Sulpicia, and Lucilius.* London: Bohn, 1852.

Feinberg, Leonard. *The Satirist, His Temperament, Motivation, and Influence.* Ames: Iowa State UP, 1963.

Fenoaltea, Doranne, and David Lee Rubin, eds. *The Ladder of High Designs: Structure and Interpretation of the French Lyric Sequence.* Charlottesville: UP of Virginia, 1991.

Flandrin, Jean-Louis. "Pour une histoire du goût." *La Cuisine et la table.* Special issue of *L'Histoire* 85 (1986): 12–19.

Fowler, Alastair. *Kinds of Literature: An Introduction to the Theory of Genres and Modes.* Cambridge: Harvard UP, 1982.

Freud, Sigmund. *Jokes and Their Relation to the Unconscious.* 1905. Vol. 8 of *The Complete Psychological Works of Sigmund Freud.* 18 vols. Trans. James Strachey. London: Hogarth, 1960.

Freudenberg, Kirk. *The Walking Muse: Horace on the Theory of Satire.* Princeton: Princeton UP, 1993.

Frye, Northrup. *Anatomy of Criticism.* Princeton: Princeton UP, 1957.

Furetière, Antoine. *Dictionnaire universel.* Hildesheim and New York: Georg Holms, 1972.

Génetiot, Alain. "L'Épître en vers mondaine de Voiture à Mme Deshoulières." *L'Épître en vers au XVIIe siècle.* Ed. Jean-Pierre Chauveau. Littératures classiques 18. Paris: Klincksieck, 1993. 103–14.

Godfrey, Sima. "The Anxiety of Anticipation: Ulterior Motives in French Poetry." *Yale French Studies* 66 (1984): 1–26.

Goubert, Pierre. *La Société.* Vol. 1 of *L'Ancien Régime.* Paris: Armand Colin, 1969.

Hampton, Timothy, ed. *Baroque Topographies: Literature/History/ Philosophy.* Special issue of *Yale French Studies* 80 (1991).

Hesiod. *Works and Days.* Oxford: Clarendon, 1978.

Highet, Gilbert. *The Anatomy of Satire.* Princeton: Princeton UP, 1962.

———. *Juvenal the Satirist: A Study.* Oxford: Clarendon, 1954.

Hodgart, Matthew. *Satire.* New York: McGraw, 1969.

Holy Bible. King James Version.

Hope, Quentin M. "Saint-Evremond and the Pleasures of the Table." *Papers on French Seventeenth Century Literature* 20 (1993): 10–36.

Horace. *The Complete Works of Horace.* Trans. Charles Passage. New York: Unger, 1983.

———. *Horace's Satires and Epistles.* Trans. Jacob Fuchs. New York: Norton, 1977.

———. *Satires, Epistles and Ars Poetica.* (Bilingual ed.) Ed. and trans. H. Rushton Fairclough. Cambridge: Harvard UP, 1926.

Huppert, George. *Les Bourgeois Gentilshommes.* Chicago: U of Chicago P, 1977.

Joret, Paul. *Nicolas Boileau-Despréaux: Révolutionnaire et conformiste.* Biblio 17 49. Paris, Seattle, and Tübingen: Papers on French Seventeenth Century Literature, 1989.

Juvenal. *The Satires of Juvenal Translated.* Trans. Thomas Sheridan. London: Browne, 1739. Rpt. New York: AMS, 1978.

Kaiser, Walter. *Praisers of Folly.* Cambridge: Harvard UP, 1963.

Kernan, Alvin B. *The Plot of Satire.* New Haven: Yale UP, 1965.

La Fontaine, Jean de. *Fables choisies mises en vers.* Ed. Georges Couton. Paris: Garnier, 1962.

Lanson, Gustave. *Boileau.* Paris: Hachette, 1892.

La Varenne, François. *Le Cuisinier françois.* Ed. J.-L. Flandrin, Philip Hyman, and Mary Hyman. Paris: Montalba, 1983.

Lawrence, Katherine D. "Rhetorical and Fictional Aspects in the *Satyres* of Mathurin Régnier." Diss. Catholic U, 1983.

Lefebvre, Joël. *Les Fols et la folie: Étude sur le genre du comique et la création littéraire en Allemagne pendant la Renaissance.* Paris: Klincksieck, 1968.

Leiner, Wolfgang. "Métamorphoses magdaléennes." *La Métamorphose dans la poésie baroque française et anglaise.* Ed. Gisèle Mathieu-Castellani. Paris: Place, 1980. 45–56.

Lough, John. *Writers and Public in France.* Oxford: Clarendon, 1978.

Lucilius. *Remains of Old Latin.* Vol. 3. Trans. E. H. Farmington. Cambridge: Harvard UP, 1957.

Mack, Maynard. "The Muse of Satire." *Yale Review* 41 (1951): 80–92.

MacKenzie, Louis A., Jr. "Three Literary Visions of Seventeenth-Century Paris." *Literary Generations: A Festschrift in Honor of Edward D. Sullivan.* Ed. Alain Toumayan. Lexington: French Forum, 1992. 98–109.

Marin, Louis. *Portrait of the King.* Trans. Martha Houle. Minneapolis: U of Minnesota P, 1988.

Miner, Earl. "Some Issues for Study of Integrated Collections." *Poems in Their Place: The Intertextuality and Order of Poetic Collections.* Ed. Neil Fraistat. Chapel Hill: U of North Carolina P, 1986.

Molière. *Œuvres complètes.* Ed. Robert Jouanny. 2 vols. Paris: Garnier, 1962.

Montaigne. *Les Essais.* Ed. Pierre Villey. Paris: PUF, 1965.

Mornet, Daniel. *L'Histoire de la littérature française classique, 1660–1700.* 3rd ed. Paris: Armand Colin, 1947.

———. *Nicolas Boileau.* Paris: Editions Calmann-Lévy, 1943.

Népote-Desmarres, Fanny. "Boileau, esprit satirique et satires en vers: Une Ontologie du verbe." *La Satire en vers au XVIIe siècle.* Ed. Louise Godard de Donville. Littératures classiques 24. Paris: Klincksieck, 1995. 183 93.

Nitze, William A., and E. Preston Dargan. *A History of French Literature.* Rev. ed. New York: Holt, 1922

Ovid. *Metamorphoses.* Baltimore: Penguin, 1961.

Persius. *The Satires.* Trans. J. R. Jenkinson. Warminster, Eng.: Aris and Phillips, 1980.

Pineau, Joseph. *L'Univers satirique de Boileau: L'Ardeur, la grâce et la loi.* Genève: Droz, 1990.

Pintard, René. *Le Libertinage érudit en France au XVIIe siècle.* 2 vols. Paris: Boivin, 1943.

Pocock, Gordon. *Boileau and the Nature of Neo-Classicism.* Cambridge: Cambridge UP, 1980.

Pope, Alexander. *The Poems of Alexander Pope.* Ed. John Butt. New Haven: Yale UP, 1963.

Randolphe, M. C. "The Structural Design of the Formal Verse Satire." *Philological Quarterly* 21 (1942): 368–84.

Régnier, Mathurin. *Œuvres complètes.* Ed. Gabriel Raibaud. Paris: Didier, 1958.

Reichler, Claude. *L'Âge libertin.* Paris: Minuit, 1987.

Révillout, Charles. "La Légende de Boileau." *Essais de philologie et de littérature.* Montpellier: Hamelin, 1899.

Rubin, David Lee. "Consciousness and the External World in a Caprice by Saint-Amant." *Yale French Studies* 49 (1973): 170–77.

———. "Icon and Caricature: Poetic Images of the Sun King." *Sun King: The Ascendancy of French Culture during the Reign of Louis XIV.* Ed. David Lee Rubin. Washington: Folger, 1992. 129–43.

Saisselin, Rémy. *The Rules of Reason and the Ruses of the Heart.* Cleveland and London: Case Western Reserve U, 1970.

Santirocco, Matthew S. *Unity and Design in Horace's Odes.* Chapel Hill: U of North Carolina P, 1986.

Schulz-Buschhaus, Ulrich. "Boileaus 'Repas ridicule,' Klassiche Satire und burleske Poetologie." *Romanistisches Jahrbuch* 32 (1981): 69–91.

Smith, Barbara Herrnstein. *Poetic Closure: A Study of How Poems End.* Chicago and London: U of Chicago P, 1968.

Swain, Barbara. *Fools and Folly.* New York: Columbia UP, 1932.

Tallemant des Réaux. *Historiettes.* Ed. A. Adam and G. Dellessault. 2 vols. Paris: Gallimard, 1961.

Théophile de Viau. *Œuvres poétiques.* Ed. Guido Saba. Paris: Bordas, 1990.

———. *Œuvres poétiques.* Ed. Jeanne Streicher. 2 vols. Genève: Droz, 1967.

Tiefenbrun, Susan. "Boileau and His Friendly Enemy: A Poetics of Satiric Criticism." *Modern Language Notes* 91 (1976): 672–97

Tobin, Ronald W. *Tarte à la crème: Comedy and Gastronomy in Molière's Theater.* Columbus: Ohio State UP, 1990.

Van Rooy, C. A. "Arrangement and Structure of Satires in Horace." *Acta Classica* 11 (1968): 38–72; 13 (1970): 7–27; 13 (1970): 45–59; 14 (1971): 67–90; 15 (1972): 37–52.

Van Sickle, J. *The Design of Virgil's Bucolics.* Rome: Eteneo & Bizzarri, 1978.

Varga, A. Kibedi. *Rhétorique et littérature: Études de structures classiques.* Paris: Didier, 1970.

Virgil. *Georgics.* New York: Oxford UP, 1947.

Voltaire. *Dictionnaire philosophique.* Paris: Garnier, 1961.

Wheaton, Barbara. *Savoring the Past: The French Kitchen and Table from 1300 to 1789.* Philadelphia: U of Pennsylvania P, 1983.

White, H. E., Jr. *Nicolas Boileau.* New York: Twayne, 1969.

Winkler, Martin M. *The Persona in Three Satires of Juvenal.* Hildesheim, Zurich, and New York: Georg Olms, 1983.

Wood, Allen G. "Boileau and Affective Response." *Cahiers du Dix-Septième Siècle* (Fall 1987): 61–73.

———. "Boileau, l'équivoque, et l'œuvre ouverte." *Ordre et contestation au temps des classiques: Actes du 21e colloque du Centre Méridional de Rencontres sur le XVIIe siècle jumelé avec le 23e colloque de la North American Society for Seventeenth Century French Literature (Marseille, 19–23 juin 1991).* Ed. R. Duchêne and P. Ronzeaud. 2 vols. Biblio 17 73. Paris, Seattle, and Tübingen: Papers on French Seventeenth Century Literature, 1992. 1: 275–85.

———. *Literary Satire and Theory: A Study of Horace, Boileau, and Pope.* New York: Garland, 1985.

———. "La Poétique de l'épître chez Boileau." *L'Épître en vers au XVIIe siècle.* Ed. Jean-Pierre Chauveau. Littératures classiques 18. Paris: Klincksieck, 1993. 289–99.

———. "The *Regent du Parnasse* and *Vraisemblance.*" *French Forum* 3 (1978): 251–62.

Index